ULTIMATE Stupidly Hard QUIZ BOOK

BBC Children's Books
Published by the Penguin Group
Penguin Books Ltd. 80 Strand, London WC2R 0RL, England
Penguin Group (Australia) Ltd, 250 Camberwell Road, Camberwell, Victoria 3124, Australia (a division of Pearson Australia Group Pty Ltd)
Canada, India, New Zealand, South Africa

Published by BBC Children's Books, 2011

Content previously published as *Top Gear Stupidly Hard Quiz Book* and *Top Gear Stupidly Hard Quiz Book v.2.* Answers correct at time of going to print.

001 - 10 9 8 7 6 5 4 3 2 1

Written by David Carr and Gill Hutchison
Designed by Dan Newman

ISBN: 978-1-40590-828-3

Printed in Great Britain

Top Gear

ULTIMATE Stupidly Hard QUIZ BOOK

Contents

Hold on, he's jumped the gun!

Contents

Could You Be The Stig?

If the time came for a new tame racing driver to be crowned, would you have the nerve, the skill and the fear of ducks to become The Stig? Take the test and find out!

1. **The colour of the next Stig would be:**

a) Red
b) Blue
c) Neon green
d) Silver

2. **You're driving an Ascari A10 at approximately 120mph on the test track when, on your approach to Hammerhead, a rear tyre blows, sending you into an uncontrollable spin. What do you do?**

a) Start screaming and signal to emergency crews to call an ambulance
b) Get a firm grip on the steering wheel and do your best to control the vehicle, hoping you don't hit the tyre wall
c) Turn up the stereo so you can hear your favourite song over the revving engine
d) Take the opportunity to get a quick nap in and let the Ascari do its own thing

3. **If you were to have a household pet to keep you company, what would it be?**

a) A cat named James
b) A hamster named Richard
c) A house plant named Steve
d) A dog named Jeremy

4. **Given the choice of listening to whatever you wanted while taking a lap in an Ariel Atom (if it actually had a radio), would you play...**

a) 'Guilty' by Barbra Streisand & Barry Gibb
b) *Spanish For Beginners* by Alfredo Cruz
c) Nothing
d) Classical baroque

5. **Where would you take your holidays while *Top Gear* is off the air?**

a) Isle of Capri, Italy
b) Silverstone, Northamptonshire
c) Majorca, Spain
d) The Bahamas

6. **What sort of car would you drive in your leisure time?**

a) What leisure time?
b) Take my pick from the *Top Gear* garage
c) Pagani Zonda F
d) Ford Focus RS

7. **The Stig has an unknown number of relatives around the world. We've already met two of them, in the USA and Botswana. Where do you expect the next member of the Family Stig to pop up?**

a) Australia: Dame Edna Everstig
b) Tibet: Dalai Stigma
c) Japan: Takashi Stig-san
d) France: Pepe Le Stig

8. **Everyone knows The Stig has a tattoo of Buzz Aldrin on his thigh. What kind of tattoo would you get to prove your Stigness?**

a) The Renault logo on your bicep
b) A flaming skull with Maserati MC12s jumping out of each eye socket across your back
c) 'Colin' above your right nipple after the founder of Lotus, Colin Chapman
d) A teddy bear with its head resting on your belly button

9. On October 26 each year, do you...

a) Do a spot of housework then watch your 'Best of Le Mans' DVD
b) Observe the anniversary of the signing of the Treaty of Ripon between Scotland and England in 1640
c) Celebrate the National Day of Austria
d) Enjoy your birthday with friends

10. Which past Grand Prix champion should a Stig try to emulate?

a) Nigel Mansell
b) Lewis Hamilton
c) Damon Hill
d) None of the above

Answers

1. a) or d) Either of these would be acceptable, not to mention completely cool
2. c) The Stig doesn't scream, pray or sleep.
3. c) Obviously.
4. c) Nothing. The Ariel Atom doesn't have a stereo.
5. b) The Stig is sentimental.
6. b) Obviously.
7. Any of these is possible.
8. b) I think we can agree the others are seriously uncool.
9. Er, that would be d.
10. d) The Stig? Emulate a Grand Prix driver? Please!

Scores

8-10: You must have 98 RON petrol running through your veins. You sure you're not related?

4-7: There's no doubt, you're ice cold. A little more time on the track, a little less chat and it's unleash The Stig!

0-3: Sorry, but the closest you're going to get to The Stig is the poster of him on your bedroom wall. Come on, you know you've got one.

Testing Times

The test track is the spiritual home of *Top Gear*. The place where reputations are made and records are broken. Keep a close eye on the clock for this challenge, but be careful – there's some tricky turns thrown in just for you.

1. How long is the *Top Gear* test track?

a) 1.5 miles (2.41 kilometres)
b) 2 miles (3.2 kilometres)
c) 2.5 miles (4 kilometres)
d) 3 miles (4.8 kilometres)

2. Where is the test track located?

a) Stigton Common
b) Salisbury Plain
c) Dunsfold Park
d) Wuthering Heights

3. What type of shape is it?

a) S-Bend
b) Figure-8
c) U-Turn
d) Wide Loop

4. How many turns are there?

a) 6
b) 12
c) 8
d) 9

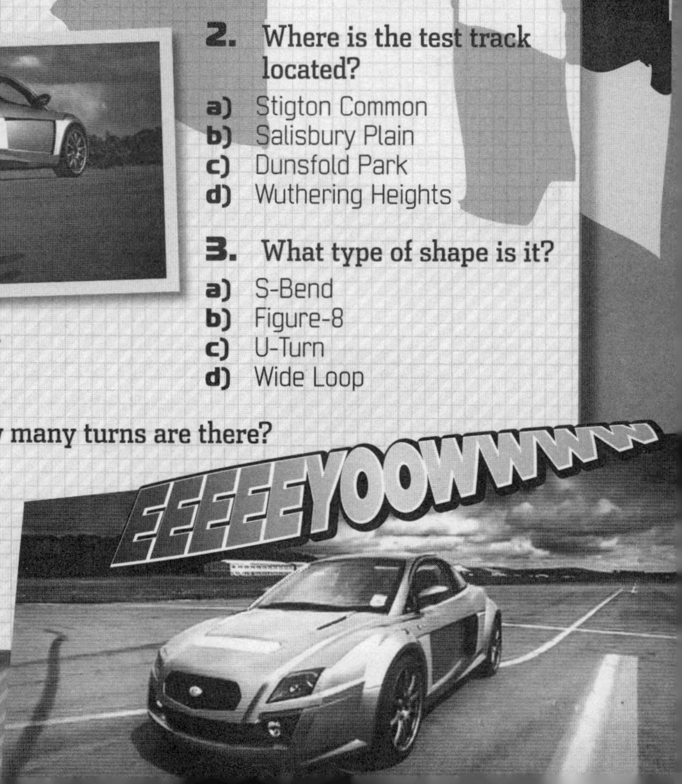

5. **What make of vehicle has done the most number of laps on the test track?**

a) Koenigsegg
b) Ferrari
c) Suzuki
d) Volkswagen

6. **Which of the following is not a section of the *Top Gear* test track?**

a) Hammerhead
b) Baltimore
c) Chicago
d) Bentley

7. **Engineers from which British car manufacturer designed the test track?**

a) Jaguar
b) Lotus
c) Rover
d) Noble

8. **Which British actor had a corner named in his honour after almost rolling the Suzuki Liana he was driving?**

a) Neil Morrissey
b) Steve Coogan
c) Alan Davies
d) Michael Gambon

9. **What is the fastest 'non-qualifying' vehicle ever to have raced on the test track?**

a) Space Shuttle
b) Ultralight aircraft
c) Apache Attack Helicopter
d) BAE Sea Harrier

10. **Which of these past and present Formula 1 drivers posted the fastest lap time on the test track?**

a) Nigel Mansell
b) Mark Webber
c) Lewis Hamilton
d) Jenson Button

Answers

1. b) 2 miles (3.2 kilometres)
2. c) Dunsfold Park (Surrey)
3. b) Figure-8
4. d) 9
5. c) Suzuki (Liana, the Reasonably-Priced Car driven by Stars)
6. b) Baltimore
7. b) Lotus
8. d) Michael Gambon
9. d) BAE Sea Harrier
10. a) Nigel Mansell (1:44.4)

Scores

8-10: Be interesting to see your time in a reasonably-priced car.

4-7: A fairly good knowledge of the twists and turns. Pity you forgot about the tyre wall

0-3: Let's just say you wouldn't be allowed on the track in a caravan!

Challenged!

True or False

Though obviously not as demanding as the big ones, mini challenges still present a tantalising opportunity for the lads to show off their skills at crashing, sinking and making a general mess. Exercise your grey matter with these 10 questions.

1. The team decided that the best driving road in the world is from Davos in Switzerland to the Stelvio Pass in Italy.

   TRUE / FALSE

2. In a challenge to drive an amphibious vehicle across the English Channel, Richard's Volkswagen Vanagon or 'Damper van' was the only successful competitor.

   TRUE / FALSE

3. A Bugatti Veyron is faster over two miles than a Eurofighter Typhoon.

TRUE / FALSE

4. In The Race Across London challenge, the team discovered the fastest way to get across London was by bicycle.

TRUE / FALSE

5. In The British Leyland challenge, James' Austin Princess came out on top and £20 in the black.

TRUE / FALSE

6. Competing in the Britcar 24 hour endurance race at Silverstone, the team finished in last place out of 59 competitors.

TRUE / FALSE

7. Jeremy, Richard and James proved it is possible to resurface a road in 24 hours.

TRUE / FALSE

8. James took the Bugatti Veyron to its top speed of 253mph at a test track in Germany.

TRUE / FALSE

9. James and Richard failed to convert a Triumph Dolomite into a space shuttle in the required amount of time.

TRUE / FALSE

10. James built a limousine out of a Saab and a Citroën, with the interior as half a Swedish sauna and half a French café.

TRUE / FALSE

Answers

1. True.
2. False. The team made the trip in Jeremy's 'Nissank'.
3. False. The Typhoon is faster by two seconds.
4. True. Ridden by Richard.
5. True.
6. False. They did rather well, all things considered, coming in 39th and third in their class.
7. True.
8. Amazing but true.
9. False. The car was a Reliant Robin and it successfully took off before crashing into a nearby hillside.
10. False. The cars were a Saab and Alfa Romeo. Half sauna, half Sistine Chapel.

Scores

8-10: It's a little scary how much you know about half-baked experiments involving cars. Keep up the good work!

4-7: Nice one. Expect a phone call the next time the lads are looking to do something really stupid.

0-3: You need to lighten up and unleash your inner boffin.

Cool Wall Odd One Out
Part I

The source of many heated arguments between Jeremy and Richard, the Cool Wall gives them the opportunity to voice their opinions on the 'coolest' and 'uncoolest' cars on offer. Now you have a chance to do the same. Pick out the odd car in the following lists. Hope you know your stuff...

1. Dodge Caliber, Honda Civic, Volvo C30, Porsche 911

2. Fiat 500, Smart ForTwo, Mercedes C-Class, Volkswagen EOS

3. Citroën C4 Picasso, Land Rover Freelander, Volvo C30, Toyota Prius

4. Vauxhall Tigra, Peugeot 207 CC, Nissan Qashqai, Dodge Caliber

5. Aston Martin V8 Vantage, Audi TT, Honda Civic, Porsche 911

6. Cadillac XLR, BMW 1-Series, Mitsubishi Evo 9, Toyota Auris

7. Lamborghini Gallardo, Ferrari P3, Mercedes CLS, Alfa Romeo Brera

8. Audi A8, Noble M15, Mazda RX8, Volkswagen Phaeton

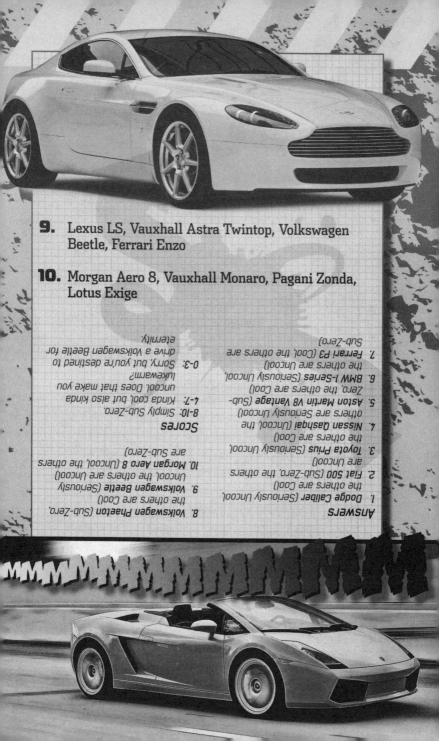

9. Lexus LS, Vauxhall Astra Twintop, Volkswagen Beetle, Ferrari Enzo

10. Morgan Aero 8, Vauxhall Monaro, Pagani Zonda, Lotus Exige

Answers

1. **Dodge Caliber** (*Seriously Uncool, the others are Cool*)
2. **Fiat 500** (*Sub-Zero, the others are Uncool*)
3. **Toyota Prius** (*Seriously Uncool, the others are Cool*)
4. **Nissan Qashqai** (*Uncool, the others are Seriously Uncool*)
5. **Aston Martin V8 Vantage** (*Sub-Zero, the others are Cool*)
6. **BMW 1-Series** (*Seriously Uncool, the others are Uncool*)
7. **Ferrari P3** (*Cool, the others are Sub-Zero*)
8. **Volkswagen Phaeton** (*Sub-Zero, the others are Cool*)
9. **Volkswagen Beetle** (*Seriously Uncool, the others are Uncool*)
10. **Morgan Aero 8** (*Uncool, the others are Sub-Zero*)

Scores

8-10: *Simply Sub-Zero.*

4-7: *Kinda cool, but also kinda uncool. Does that make you lukewarm?*

0-3: *Sorry, but you're destined to drive a Volkswagen Beetle for eternity.*

Stars in Reasonably-Priced Cars

Glittering international celebrities they may be, but out on the *Top Gear* test track our Stars in Reasonably-Priced Cars are mere putty in the hands of The Stig; whose task it is to turn them into hardened racing machines. It works – sometimes. See if you can score better than many of our visiting celebs in this quick quiz...

1. Who was the first ever celebrity guest on *Top Gear*, appearing in Episode 1 on 20 October, 2002?

a) Neil Morrissey
b) Joanna Lumley
c) David Soul
d) Harry Enfield

2. Three different makes of car have been driven by celebrities around the *Top Gear* test track, the Suzuki Liana, the Chevrolet Lacetti and the Kia Cee'd. Who is the fastest in each car?

____

3. How many females are in the top ten on the Lacetti leader board?

a) 1
b) 2
c) 3
d) 4

4. How many celebrity chefs have driven around the test track?

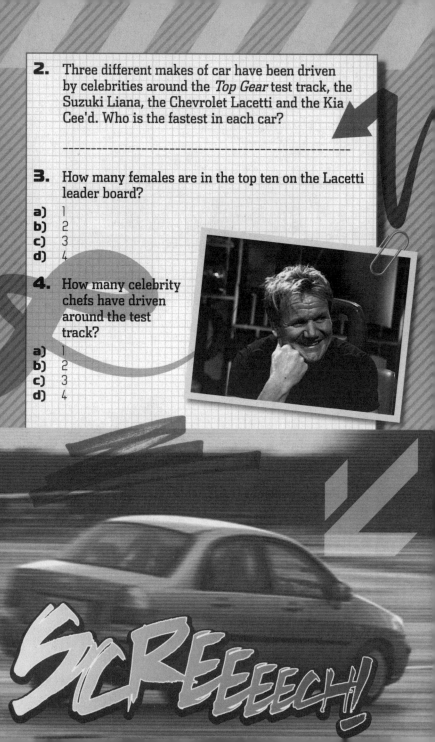

a) 1
b) 2
c) 3
d) 4

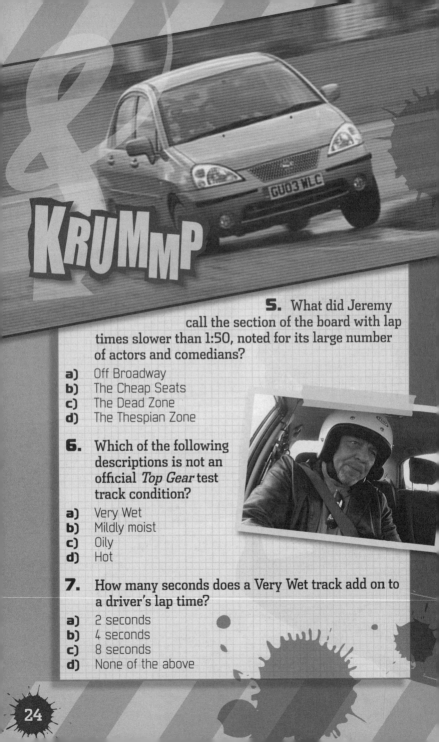

5. What did Jeremy call the section of the board with lap times slower than 1:50, noted for its large number of actors and comedians?

a) Off Broadway
b) The Cheap Seats
c) The Dead Zone
d) The Thespian Zone

6. Which of the following descriptions is not an official *Top Gear* test track condition?

a) Very Wet
b) Mildly moist
c) Oily
d) Hot

7. How many seconds does a Very Wet track add on to a driver's lap time?

a) 2 seconds
b) 4 seconds
c) 8 seconds
d) None of the above

8. Who played Obi-Wan Kenobi in the Star Wars movies and posted a time of 1:48.0 in the Lacetti?

---

9. How many Doctor Whos have completed lap times in a Reasonably-Priced Car?

a) 1
b) 2
c) 3
d) None

10. Several football players have tested their driving skills on the track. Name two of them.

Answers

1. **d)** Harry Enfield
2. Dame Ellen MacArthur (Liana), Simon Cowell (Lacetti) (half point each) and Rowan Atkinson.
3. **a)** 1 (Jennifer Saunders)
4. **b)** 2 (Jamie Oliver and Gordon Ramsay)
5. **d)** The Thespian Zone
6. **c)** Oily
7. **d)** None of the above. A Very Wet track can cost a driver around 6 seconds.
8. Ewan McGregor
9. **b)** 2 (Christopher Eccleston and David Tennant)
10. Ian Wright, Vinnie Jones, or Les Ferdinand

Scores

8-10: So where'd you park your Reasonably-Priced Car?
4-7: There's more to celebs than what you read in the tabloids. Must try harder.
0-3: They're famous. That means you're supposed to know who they are.

Winter Olympics Special

True or False

For something entirely different, the producers decided to send the team to Norway for a series of Winter Olympic-sized challenges in and around Lillehammer. They figured the cold might slow them down a bit. It didn't. Question is, how slow are you going to be getting through these teasers?

1. Jeremy challenged James to a cross country driving and shooting biathlon, the loser of which had to eat 'golden snow'.

TRUE / FALSE

I **don't** want to **eat golden snow!**

2. James was the one who had to eat the golden snow.

TRUE / FALSE

3. Jeremy raced a Jaguar XK8 against a speed skater on an ice course and won by three seconds.

TRUE / FALSE

4. James again beat Jeremy, this time in a race on a frozen lake.

TRUE / FALSE

5. Jeremy lost when the Jaguar he was driving spun off into a snow bank and got stuck.

TRUE / FALSE

6. Richard took on James in a race between a bobsleigh and a rally car. Richard was in the rally car and terrified.

TRUE / FALSE

7. The bobsleigh again took the checkered flag, by three seconds.

TRUE / FALSE

8. In a game of five-a-side hockey, ten Ford Mondeos knocked a puck around the ice.

TRUE / FALSE

I've won a *Top Gear* challenge!

9. Miraculously, with a little help from Jeremy, James' team won the match.

TRUE / FALSE

10. With some assistance from the United Kingdom Rocketry Association, the team strapped rockets to the back of a local Norwegian car and sent it down a ski-jump, in an attempt to beat the distance set by a ski-jumper.

TRUE / FALSE

Answers

1. True
2. False. Incredibly, James won. And somehow, Jeremy avoided the unpleasant task.
3. False. With no grip on the surface, Jeremy was lapped twice and easily beaten.
4. True
5. True
6. False. He rode the bobsleigh.
7. True
8. False. The cars were Suzuki Swifts.
9. False. Richard's team won 5-4.
10. False. They strapped the rockets to the back of a Mini.

Scores

8-10: Nice one, Sven. Clearly you've spent a bit of time in the Nordic regions.

4-7: If this were the alpine decathlon you'd be on track for a bronze. Oh dear.

0-3: Sorry, but it's the golden snow for you, friend.

Just Jeremy

True or False

When you're dealing with someone like Jeremy Clarkson, a man known around the world for his love of brash statements, spotting the falsehoods in this lot is going to be tough indeed. Good luck!

1. In the first amphibious vehicle challenge, Jeremy renames his Nissan, 'Nissank'.

   TRUE / FALSE

2. He proved that it is possible to drive a Volkswagen Golf up a Scottish mountain.

   TRUE / FALSE

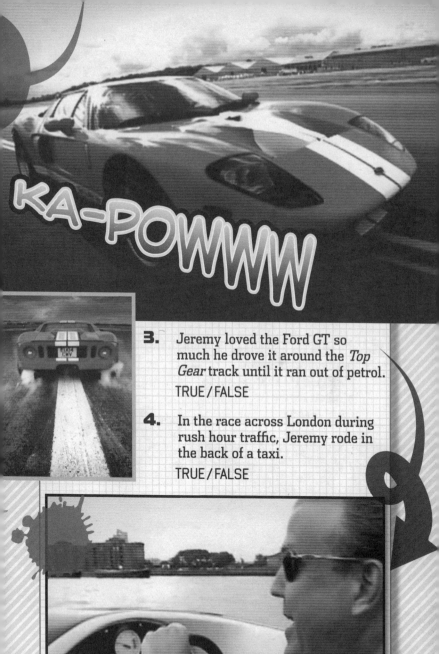

3. Jeremy loved the Ford GT so much he drove it around the *Top Gear* track until it ran out of petrol.

TRUE / FALSE

4. In the race across London during rush hour traffic, Jeremy rode in the back of a taxi.

TRUE / FALSE

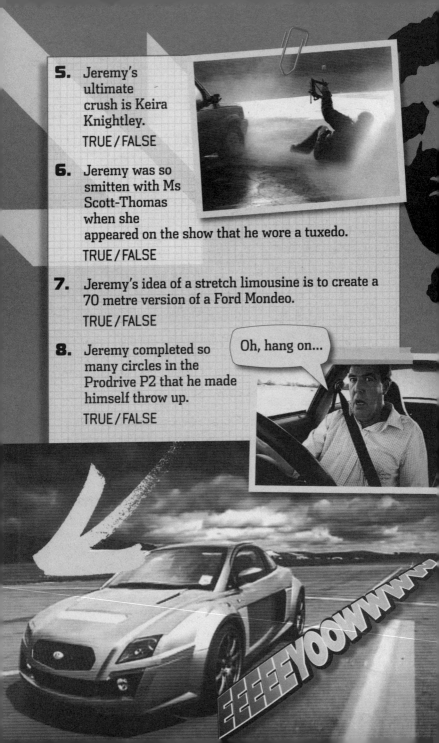

5. Jeremy's ultimate crush is Keira Knightley.

TRUE / FALSE

6. Jeremy was so smitten with Ms Scott-Thomas when she appeared on the show that he wore a tuxedo.

TRUE / FALSE

7. Jeremy's idea of a stretch limousine is to create a 70 metre version of a Ford Mondeo.

TRUE / FALSE

8. Jeremy completed so many circles in the Prodrive P2 that he made himself throw up.

TRUE / FALSE

9. He managed to outmanoeuvre an Apache Attack chopper.

TRUE / FALSE

10. And in a simulated battle with a Challenger 2 tank, he also survived unscathed.

TRUE / FALSE

Answers

1. False. This was the name of his vehicle in the second challenge.
2. False. The car was a Land Rover Discovery.
3. True
4. False. He drove a powerboat up the Thames.
5. False. Close but that honour would have to go to Kristin Scott Thomas.
6. False. A suit perhaps, but nothing as flash as a tux.
7. False. He stretched a Fiat Panda.
8. True. It wasn't pretty.
9. True. For a while. Before it locked its guns on him.
10. False

Scores

8-10: Your knowledge of Clarkson is spot on. And you're just like him. Always right!

4-7: Given how predictable the man is, it's surprising you didn't do better.

0-3: As Jeremy would say, 'It's all gone horribly wrong!'

Some Say...

...he is confused by stairs and that his brain is a satellite navigation system. Who can be sure? But while his personal life may be a mystery, there are some very public things we know about Colonel Fotherington Digby-Stigby. What do you know?

1. According to Jeremy, what disorder does The Stig suffer from?

a) Webbered Feet
b) Jenson's Buttocks
c) Mansell Syndrome
d) Hamilton Hands

2. How did The Black Stig perish, causing the creation of The White Stig?

a) He drank biofuel
b) He drove off an aircraft carrier
c) His head was crushed in a freak electric sunroof accident
d) He lives!

3. Which Formula 1 racing driver was presented with a T-shirt that stated 'I Am The Stig'?

a) Mark Webber
b) Jenson Button
c) Nigel Mansell
d) Lewis Hamilton

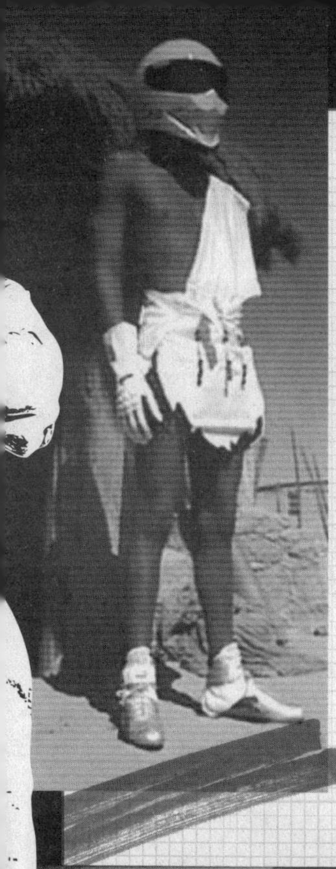

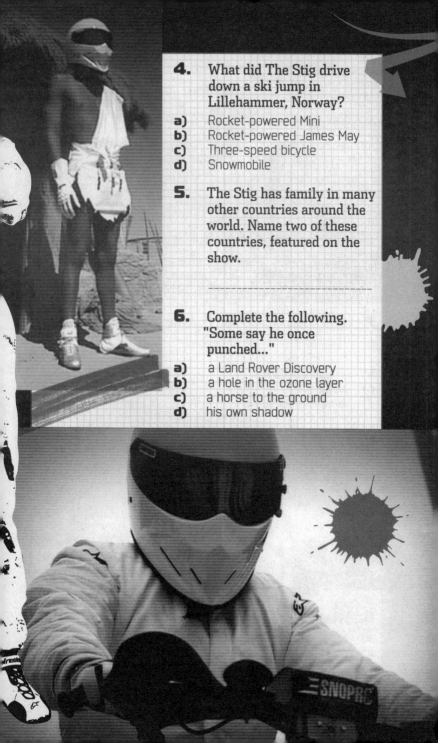

4. **What did The Stig drive down a ski jump in Lillehammer, Norway?**

a) Rocket-powered Mini
b) Rocket-powered James May
c) Three-speed bicycle
d) Snowmobile

5. **The Stig has family in many other countries around the world. Name two of these countries, featured on the show.**

----

6. **Complete the following. "Some say he once punched..."**

a) a Land Rover Discovery
b) a hole in the ozone layer
c) a horse to the ground
d) his own shadow

7. What make of car did The Stig famously spin off the *Top Gear* test track?

a) Koenigsegg CCX
b) Pagani Zonda F
c) Noble M15
d) All of the above

8. What's The Stig's favourite genre of driving music?

a) Prog rock
b) Power ballads
c) Baroque
d) All of the above

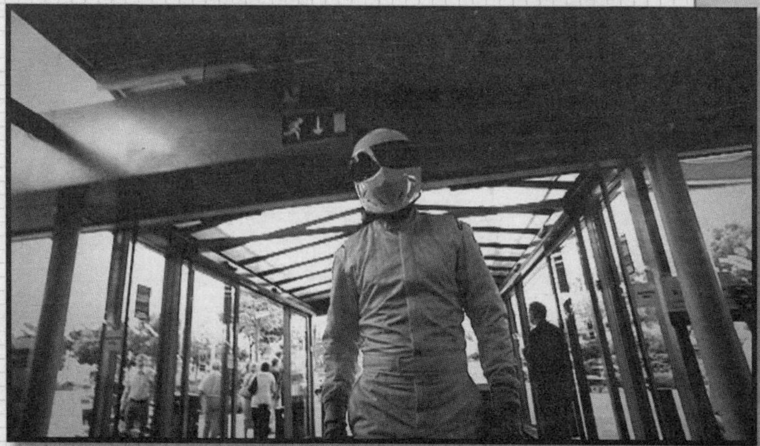

9. **What car was The Stig driving when he was pulled over by Scottish police officers?**

a) Aston Martin DBS
b) Ascari KZ1
c) TVR Sagaris
d) Caterham Seven

10. **Who is The Stig?**

a) Gordon Brown
b) Richard Hammond
c) Madonna
d) Don't ask stupid questions

Answers

1. c) Mansell Syndrome.
2. b) He drove off an aircraft carrier.
3. a) Mark Webber.
4. d) Snowmobile.
5. Botswana and the USA.
6. c) a horse to the ground.
7. a) Koenigsegg CCX.
8. d) All of the above.
9. d) Caterham Seven kit car.
10. d) Don't ask stupid questions.

Scores

8-10: (Silence. You have pleased The Stig.)
4-7: Perhaps you're not as Stig-like as you think you are.
0-3: The last time The Stig was upset he came to grief on an aircraft carrier. Do you really want to upset him again?

The African Challenge

True or False

The drive across Botswana was one of the lads' most challenging motoring treks and proved to be a gruelling test of second-hand vehicles and a little trying for the *Top Gear* team. Which of these survived? Who won the race? And will the lads ever be able to get the dust out of their clothing? Test your memory of the challenge with these questions.

1. Jeremy chose a Mercedes Benz 230E for the trek across Botswana.
TRUE / FALSE

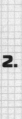

2. Richard named his car Oliver.
TRUE / FALSE

3. If any of the three vehicles chosen by the lads broke down along the journey, the driver would be forced to complete the trip in a Volvo 760.
TRUE / FALSE

4. The Makgadikgadi is a massive stretch of land with a surface composed mostly of salt.

TRUE / FALSE

5. In order to defend himself from the ferocious creatures of the Okavango Delta, Jeremy used leftover cardboard boxes to cover the passenger-side door of his car.

TRUE / FALSE

6. After crossing a river, Jeremy and James drained the water from their cars using a bucket and hose.

TRUE / FALSE

7. The lads' journey was across a part of Botswana known as the 'spine of Africa'.

TRUE / FALSE

8. Richard left a cow's head in James' tent, only to realise later that it was his own tent.

TRUE / FALSE

9. The lads enlisted the help of the Deputy Prime Minister of Botswana to test drive their safari vehicles.

TRUE / FALSE

10. The border of Botswana and South Africa signalled the end of the African challenge.

TRUE / FALSE

Answers

1. False. Jeremy's car was the 1981 Lancia Beta Coupe.
2. Sad but true.
3. False. The car was the dreaded Volkswagen Beetle.
4. True
5. False. He used aluminium cans.
6. False. They used a shotgun.
7. True
8. True
9. False. They called on Stig's African cousin.
10. False. The border of Botswana and Namibia.

Scores

8-10: The people of Botswana salute you and name a tree in your honour.

4-7: Just like driving across the Makgadikgadi – patchy.

0-3: You sure you didn't accidentally drive into Zimbabwe?

Power Lappin'

Our tame racing driver has run many a supercar through its paces on the track. Now it's your turn to put your memory to the test with these 10 Power Lap posers.

1. Which of the following cars is in the top ten of the *Top Gear* Power Board?

a) Gumpert Apollo S
b) Caterham Seven Superlight R500
c) McLaren MP4-12C
d) Ferrari 458 Italia

2. One make of car has two cars in the top ten. Can you name it?

a) Ferrari
b) Bugatti
c) Koenigsegg
d) Ascari

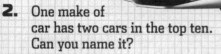

3. **What is currently sitting in last place on the Power Board?**

a) Aston Martin DB5
b) Bowler Wildcat
c) Ford Mondeo ST220
d) Porsche Pain Au Chocolat

4. **What model of Lamborghini is currently the fastest on the Power Board?**

a) Aventador LP 700-4
b) Murciélago LP670-4 SuperVeloce
c) Reventón
d) Miura

5. **Which country designs and manufactures the Koenigsegg?**

a) Denmark
b) Czech Republic
c) Italy
d) Sweden

6. **Which car is in first place on the Power Board?**

a) Pagani Zonda F
b) Maserati MC12
c) Ariel AtomV8 500
d) Lamborghini Murciélago

7. **What does the 'F' stand for in Pagani Zonda F?**

a) Fast
b) Fabulous
c) Fangio
d) Ferrari-chaser

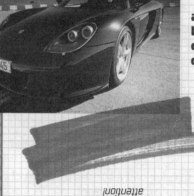

8. **Which car in the top ten has a lot of speed but not a lot of body work?**

a) Mercedes McLaren
b) Ariel Atom
c) Porsche Carrera GT
d) Noble M15

9. **Which of these makes of car has never made it onto the Power Board?**

a) Toyota
b) Mazda
c) Cadillac
d) Bentley

10. **Which car has appeared the most on the Power Board?**

a) Ferrari
b) Mercedes
c) Lamborghini
d) Porsche

Answers

1. **d)** Ferrari 458 Italia
2. **b)** Bugatti
3. **a)** Porsche Pain Au Chocolat (18,370)
4. **b)** Murciélago LP670-4 SuperVeloce
5. **d)** Sweden
6. **c)** Ariel AtomV8 500
7. **c)** Fangio. After the legendary racing champion, Juan Manuel Fangio.
8. **b)** Ariel Atom
9. **a)** Toyota
10. **d)** Porsche (nine times)

Scores

8-10: Fantastic. The Ferrari Enzo of quiz scores!
4-7: Not bad. Perhaps the awesome speeds made you dizzy.
0-3: OK, so they're quick, but pay attention!

How Hard Can It Be?

True or False

Mostly impossible. But if you think that's going to prevent Jeremy, Richard and James from attempting some of the most hair-brained challenges ever seen on television, think again.

1. A convertible people carrier can successfully travel at 100mph without losing its canvas roof.

TRUE / FALSE

2. And it will, if a *Top Gear* presenter has anything to do with it, cause a fire in a car wash.

TRUE / FALSE

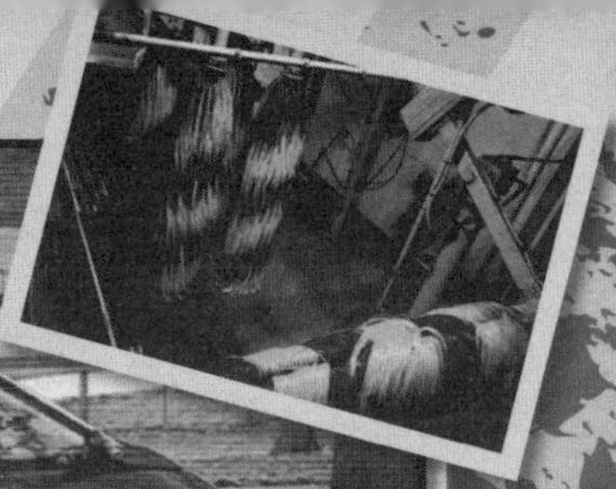

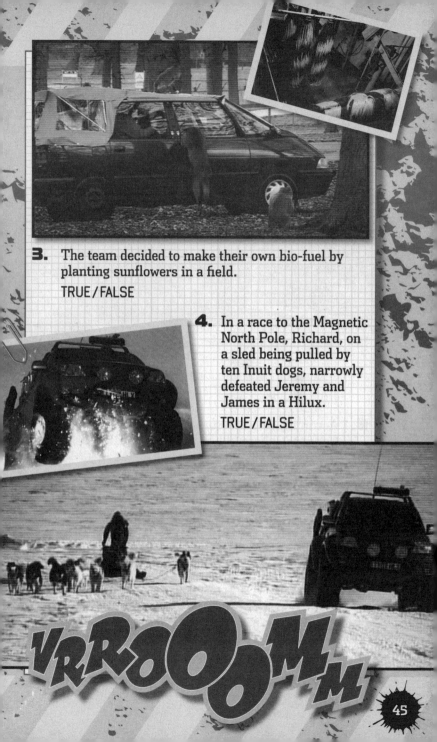

3. The team decided to make their own bio-fuel by planting sunflowers in a field.

TRUE / FALSE

4. In a race to the Magnetic North Pole, Richard, on a sled being pulled by ten Inuit dogs, narrowly defeated Jeremy and James in a Hilux.

TRUE / FALSE

VRROOOMMM

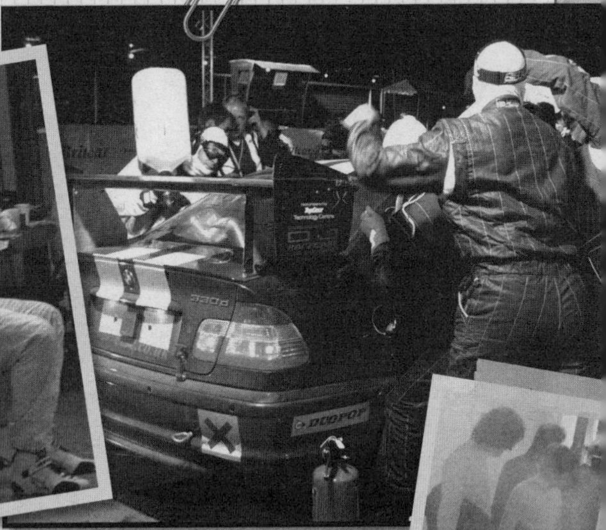

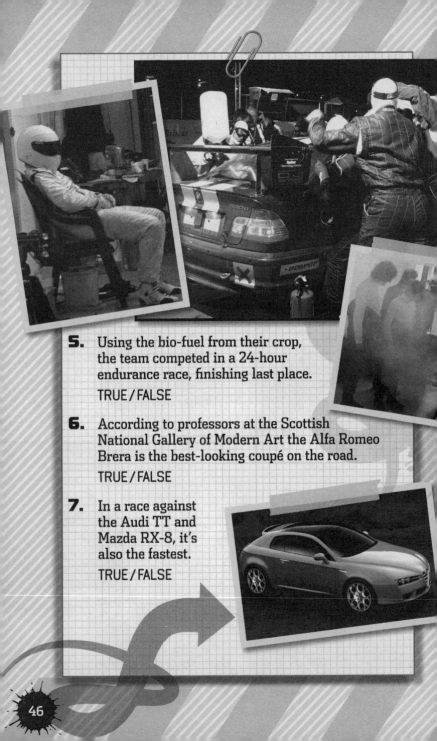

5. Using the bio-fuel from their crop, the team competed in a 24-hour endurance race, finishing last place.

TRUE / FALSE

6. According to professors at the Scottish National Gallery of Modern Art the Alfa Romeo Brera is the best-looking coupé on the road.

TRUE / FALSE

7. In a race against the Audi TT and Mazda RX-8, it's also the fastest.

TRUE / FALSE

8. Jeremy completed a lap of the infamous Nürburgring in under 10 minutes.

TRUE / FALSE

9. German former motor racing driver Sabine Schmitz later beat Jeremy's time in a Ford Transit van.

TRUE / FALSE

10. Jeremy, Richard and James are guaranteed lucrative careers as drive time radio presenters.

TRUE / FALSE

Answers

1. True. Just.
2. True. Incredible, but true.
3. False. They planted rapeseed.
4. False. Jeremy and James won that race.
5. False. They finished 39th overall
6. True
7. False. The Audi TT won.
8. True
9. False. She got very close though, taking the shine off Jeremy's time.
10. False. Very false.

Scores

8-10: You consider yourself a bit of a mad professor, don't you?

4-7: What do you mean driving an amphibious vehicle across the English Channel is crazy?

0-3: Come on admit it. You like going on caravan holidays, don't you?

Top Gear Highway Code

Anyone wishing to drive on British roads must pass a theory test, covering general rules, road safety, hazards, signage and more. However, when the *Top Gear* team cast an eye over the contents, they noticed some glaring omissions. So, in order to provide a more rounded overview of what to expect when out on the road, they put together the *Top Gear* Highway Code Questionnaire; an essential document designed to fill the gaps missing from the so-called 'official' version. See how you go with the following questions...

1. The maximum speed you can drive on a UK motorway when towing a caravan is 60mph. What is the maximum speed you can drive when attempting to jump five caravans in a Volvo 240 Estate?

a) 60 mph
b) 70 mph
c) None of the above. A Volvo 240 Estate would never go that fast.

2. In the diagram below, the amphibious 'Damper van' is looking to make a left turn at the roundabout. The Triumph Herald 'sailboat' however, coming from the opposite direction, wants to turn right. Which driver's hairstyle is bigger than their vehicles?

a) The short bloke in the 'Damper van'.
b) The guy in the 'sailboat' with the big hair.
c) They both have ridiculously big hair.

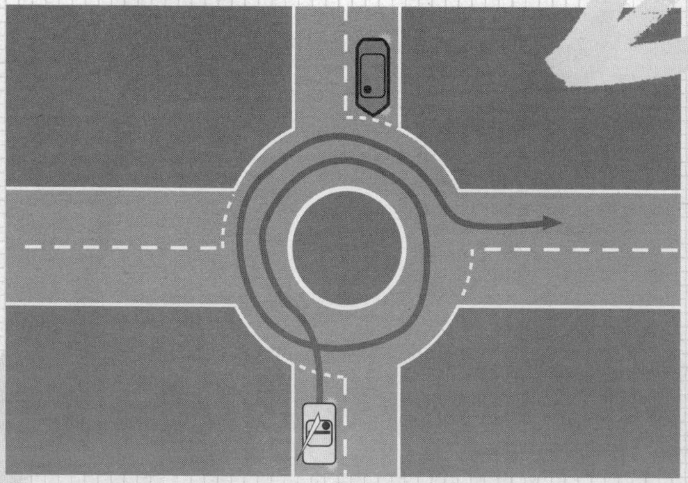

3. **What is the curb to curb turning circle of a Fiat Panda stretch limo?**

a) 50 feet.
b) 150 feet.
c) Cannot answer since it hasn't finished turning.

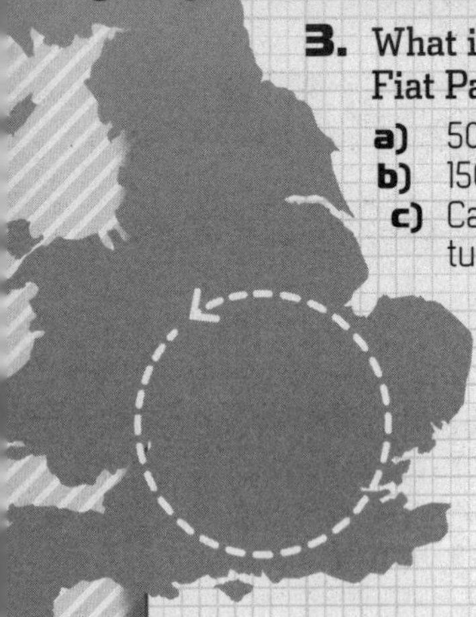

4. **Imagine you are driving the high-performance Maserati MC12 supercar, when you come across a 'toucan crossing'. How is a 'toucan crossing' different from other crossings?**

a) Cyclists can use it.
b) There is a flashing light.
c) They are manned by toucans.

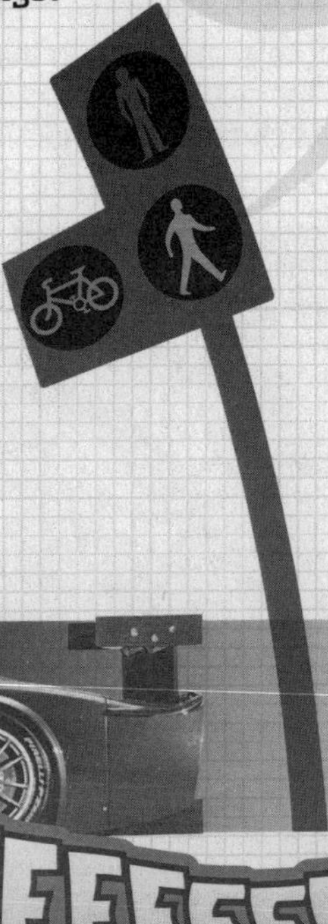

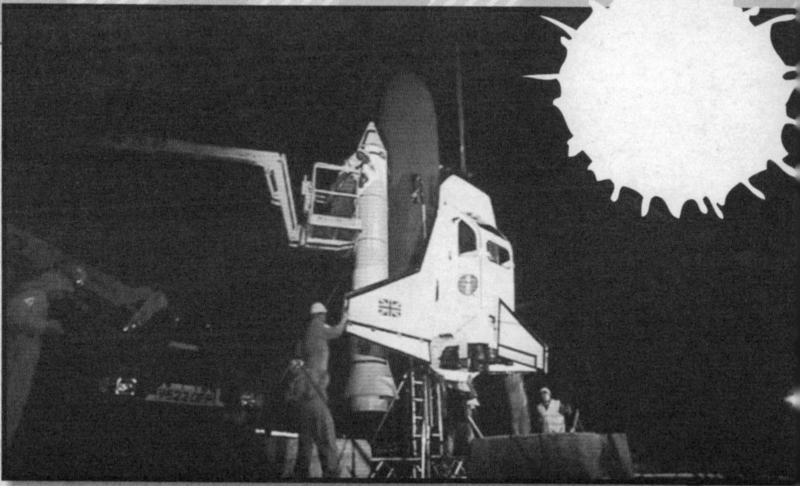

5. **Before moving off from the parked position in a modified Reliant Robin, you should first:**

a) Fasten your seatbelt.
b) Check blind spots for other road users.
c) Look up to the sky and think, 'Onwards and upwards!'

6. **Look at the images below. What is the minimum safe stopping distance for this vehicle?**

a) 80 metres.
b) Three and a half miles.
c) France.

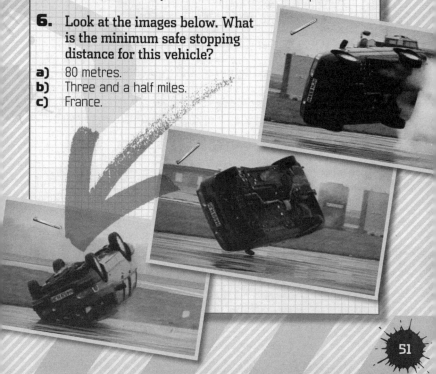

7. **Choose the most appropriate outcome in this situation:**

a) The driver allows the pedestrian to cross safely before moving on.

b) The driver hails the pedestrian and gives him a map for a different city, thus confusing the pedestrian and allowing the driver to win the race.

c) The pedestrian, aware that the car is being driven by an ultra-competitive television presenter, allows the driver to move on, then calls a taxi.

8. **Before overtaking in Iceland you should always:**

a) Signal to the other vehicle by creating an impressive arc of water with the rear of your car.

b) Pass at a safe speed, but fast enough so as to avoid sinking.

c) Check your blind spot for marine mammals.

9. In the image below, circle which objects are in the driver's blind spot:

10. What does this sign mean?

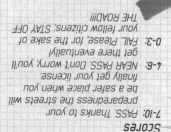

a) No entry for vehicles carrying explosives.

b) You perhaps ought to check the roof of your car.

c) *Top Gear* film crew in area.

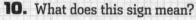

Answers

1. c)
2. c)
3. c)
4. a)
5. c)
6. a)
7. Any answer is suitable.
8. b)
9. The motorcyclist.
10. a)

Scores

7-10: PASS. Thanks to your preparedness the streets will be a safer place when you finally get your license.

4-6: NEAR PASS. Don't worry, you'll get there eventually!

0-3: FAIL. Please, for the sake of your fellow citizens, STAY OFF THE ROAD!!!

Hamster Tales

True or False

Always up for a race against his fellow hosts, Richard is the go-to guy of the team when a theory needs to be put to the test. Or is he? Try your hand at these true or false teasers.

1. In a drag race against Jeremy in an Audi R8, Richard, in his own Porsche 911 Carrera 2S, lost by 3.1 seconds.

   TRUE / FALSE

2. In the African Challenge, Richard's Opel Kadett was the only car to not shed any weight for the drive across the Makgadikgadi salt pan.

   TRUE / FALSE

3. Richard revealed he tried to have the Opel shipped over to the UK but British Customs would not allow it.

   TRUE / FALSE

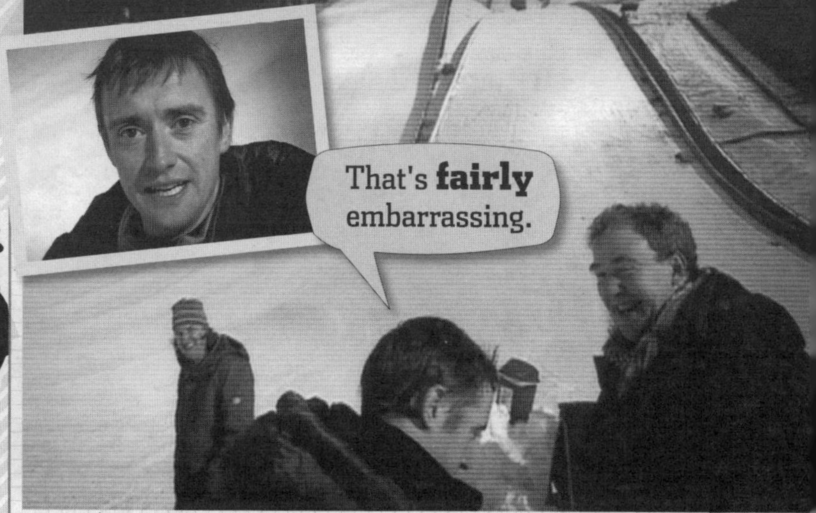
That's **fairly** embarrassing.

4. Richard won the 'Worst Dressed Presenter Award' in 2007 for wearing bicycle shorts in the Race Across London.

TRUE / FALSE

5. Richard Hammond's great grandfather invented the Hammond organ.

TRUE / FALSE

6. When Richard tried to add a Ducati 1098 motorcycle to the Cool Wall, Jeremy removed it with a chainsaw.

TRUE / FALSE

7. Given the task of stopping the rocket-powered Mini at the end of the Lillehammer ski-jump, Richard placed the barrier on the wrong run.

TRUE / FALSE

8. Richard got his nickname 'Hamster', after it was revealed he used to race the furry creatures as a child.

TRUE/FALSE

9. Richard has never won the Nobel Prize for Really Excellent Challenges.

TRUE/FALSE

10. In a fight with Jeremy over the placement of the BMW M6 on the Cool Wall, Richard ate the picture of the car.

TRUE/FALSE

Answers

1. False. The slow-motion replay revealed Richard's Porsche beat Jeremy in the Audi.
2. True
3. False. Richard successfully adopted Oliver the Opel, who now sits proudly in one of his many garages.
4. False. Jeremy beat him with his drysuit.
5. False. Of course not!
6. True. Jeremy doesn't like motorcycles.
7. True. Sad but true.
8. False
9. True
10. True. Hamsters eat cardboard.

Scores

8-10: Spookily good. Is your name Richard?

4-7: The thing is, how can you be sure your answers were wrong?

0-3: A poor effort. True or true?

Indestrucktible Hilux

The trusty red Toyota Hilux withstood test after test put to it and now sits proudly aloft in the *Top Gear* studio. How many metal-crunching moments from the destructive challenge can you recall?

1. **In which city did Jeremy begin his systematic destruction of the Toyota Hilux pick-up truck?**

a) Norwich
b) Bristol
c) Oxford
d) Manchester

2. **What was the first test he put the big red truck through?**

a) He ran it into a tree
b) He hit it with a spade
c) He drove it down a flight of stairs
d) He called it a sissy

3. **What did Jeremy then drive the Hilux into, causing environmentalists to phone in and complain; not to mention causing distress among the yokels?**

a) A statue
b) A tree
c) A caravan
d) A park bench

4. **Jeremy decided a good drowning would do the trick and chose which famous waterway to dowse the Hilux?**

a) River Thames
b) English Channel
c) Severn Estuary
d) Huddersfield Narrow

5. **What is this particul**

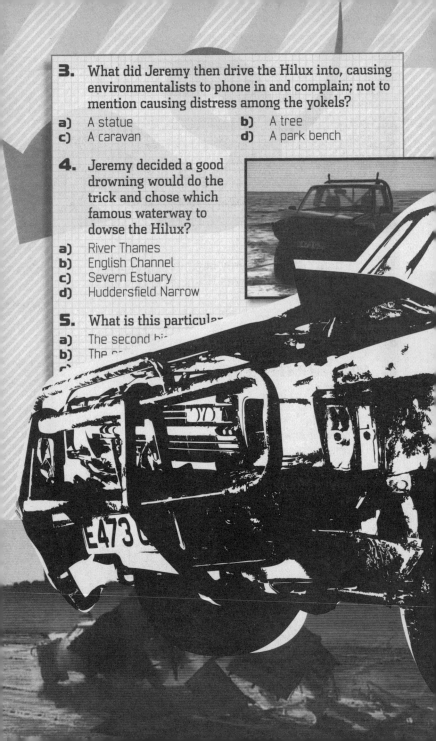

a) The second hi
b) The s

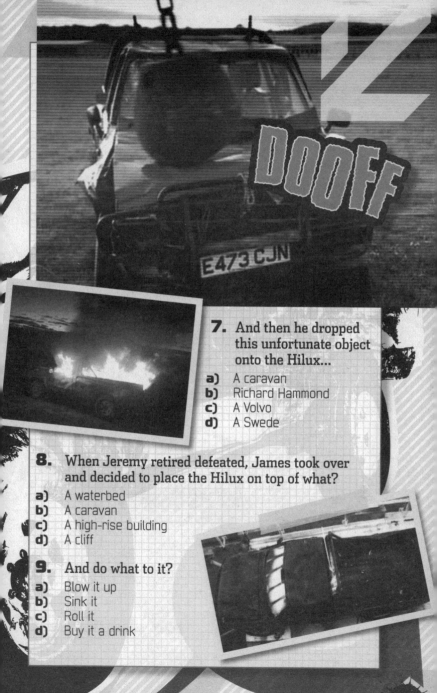

7. **And then he dropped this unfortunate object onto the Hilux...**

a) A caravan
b) Richard Hammond
c) A Volvo
d) A Swede

8. **When Jeremy retired defeated, James took over and decided to place the Hilux on top of what?**

a) A waterbed
b) A caravan
c) A high-rise building
d) A cliff

9. **And do what to it?**

a) Blow it up
b) Sink it
c) Roll it
d) Buy it a drink

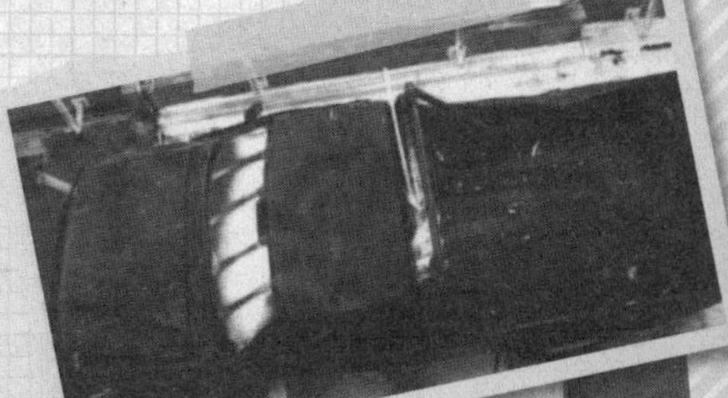

10. **Miraculously, the Hilux survived every attempt to destroy it, proving that all you need to keep the mighty pick-up going is a basic toolkit and a can of _____?**

a) Tuna
b) WD-40
c) UB-40
d) Oil

CHUG CHUGGA BRRRMMM

Answers

1. b) Bristol
2. c) He drove it down a flight of stairs.
3. b) A tree
4. c) Severn Estuary
5. a) The second biggest tide in the world.
6. d) Top Gear production office
7. a) A caravan
8. c) A high-rise building
9. a) Blow it up
10. b) WD-40

Scores

8-10: Great stuff. You must really hate pick-up trucks.
4-7: Not a total car wreck.
0-3: Lament not your lowly score, for you are a friend of the indestructible Hilux.

Battered Cars

Though perhaps not as badly treated as the Hilux, many innocent cars have suffered at the hands of the lads. Brutal maybe, but these incidents of vehicular violence have given us some classic *Top Gear* moments. For instance...

1. In a race against a skydiver in the Cypriot countryside, Richard smashed up the front of what type of off-road vehicle?

a) Land Rover Discovery
b) Volvo XC90
c) Toyota Hilux
d) Porsche Cayenne

2. In a test to gauge the power of two jet engines on a 747, Richard successfully sent a Citroën 2CV and a Ford ______ flying through the air.

a) Taurus
b) GT
c) Mondeo
d) SportKa

3. In a game of car darts, which car did James and Richard manage to get closest to the caravan bullseye?

a) Volkswagen Beetle
b) Vauxhall Carlton
c) Renault Megane
d) Vauxhall Astra

4. Environmentally-friendly and emission-free, this G-Wiz had what put into it to boost its power?

a) Engines
b) People
c) Sparkplugs
d) Batteries

5. What year was the Lancia Beta Coupe Jeremy drove in Botswana?

a) 1980
b) 1981
c) 1982
d) 1983

6. **In an effort to prove his point that Korean and Malaysian cars are terrible, Jeremy created a working vehicle out of what?**

a) Marshmallows
b) Ice cream sticks
c) Household appliances
d) Bicycles

7. **Already broken down when James purchased it, which make of Italian supercar broke down outside of Slough, causing an embarrassing traffic jam?**

a) Ferrari 308GT4
b) Maserati Merak
c) Lamborghini Urraco
d) Fiat 128

8. **What '80s classic was burnt with the fiery exhaust of a drag racer?**

a) Nissan Sunny
b) Volkswagen Beetle
c) Hyundai Coupe
d) Peugeot 206

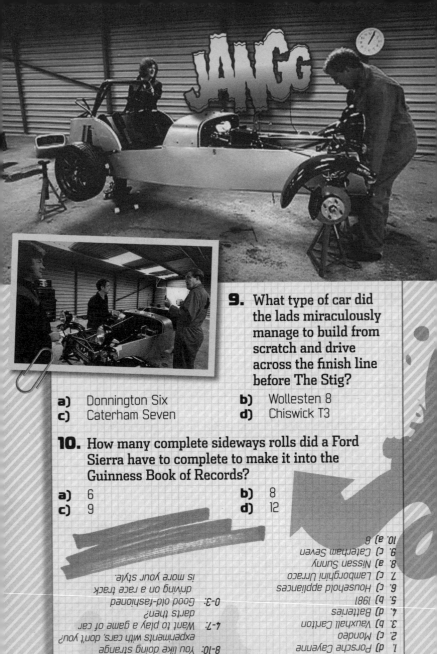

9. **What type of car did the lads miraculously manage to build from scratch and drive across the finish line before The Stig?**

a) Donnington Six
b) Wollesten 8
c) Caterham Seven
d) Chiswick T3

10. **How many complete sideways rolls did a Ford Sierra have to complete to make it into the Guinness Book of Records?**

a) 6
b) 8
c) 9
d) 12

Answers

1. d) Porsche Cayenne
2. c) Mondeo
3. b) Vauxhall Carlton
4. d) Batteries
5. b) 1981
6. c) Household appliances
7. c) Lamborghini Urraco
8. a) Nissan Sunny
9. c) Caterham Seven
10. a) 6

Scores

8-10: You like doing strange experiments with cars, don't you?
4-7: Want to play a game of car darts then?
0-3: Good old-fashioned driving on a race track is more your style.

Some Also Say...

...his earwax tastes like Turkish Delight and that if set alight he'd burn for a thousand days. All we know is that he's called The Stig. How much do you know about our tame racing driver?

1. **Complete the following. "Some say his heart..."**

a) was constructed using spent nuclear fuel
b) ticks like a watch
c) is cold like the deepest, darkest recesses of space
d) holds the key to the whereabouts of the Holy Grail

2. **"And that his ears..."**

a) are in the shape of the Nürburgring
b) don't exist
c) aren't exactly where you'd expect them to be
d) are pretty normal

3. **What was the first Stig driving when he flew off the deck of the HMS Invincible?**

a) Jaguar XJS
b) Lotus Exige S
c) Roush Mustang
d) Chevrolet Corvette

4. **Which make of car, the most powerful production vehicle ever featured on *Top Gear* (but never driven around the test track) causes The Stig to salivate from the ears whenever it is mentioned?**

a) Aston Martin ZZT
b) Porsche Wildcat
c) Bugatti Veyron
d) Bowler GT3 RS

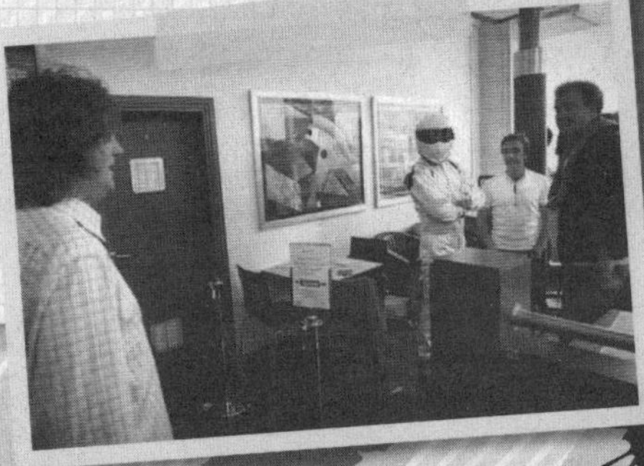

5. **The Stig's fastest official power lap time is 1 min 17.3 secs. In what car did he record this time?**

a) Koenisgsegg CCX
b) Ariel AtomV8 500
c) Maserati MC12
d) None of the above

6. **The Stig also posted the fastest lap time in the Suzuki Liana. What was his lap time?**

a) 1 min 44.4 secs
b) 3 min 30 secs
c) 4 minutes (in reverse)
d) None of the above

7. **Which of the following titles has never been used to describe The Stig?**

a) Stigless Bader
b) This Little Stiggy
c) His Holiness The Stig
d) Barbara Stighouse

8. **What make of car, driven by Jeremy, did The Stig's African cousin refuse to drive when the team visited Botswana?**

a) Volkswagen Beetle
b) Lancia Beta Coupe
c) Toyota Hilux
d) Holden Monaro

9. What was the nickname given to The Stig's American cousin?

a) Chubby Chevy
b) The Spare Tyre
c) Big Stig
d) Fat Shelby

10. Where does The Stig live?

a) In a lavishly furnished apartment behind the *Top Gear* studio
b) In a fortress of solitude deep within the Arctic Circle
c) Clapham
d) 20,000 leagues under the sea

Answers

1. **b)** *Ticks like a watch.*
2. **c)** *Aren't exactly where you'd* **expect** *them to be.*
3. **a)** *Jaguar XJS*
4. **c)** *Bugatti Veyron*
5. **b)** *Ariel Atom V8 500*
6. **a)** *1 min 44.4 secs*
7. **b)** *This Little Stiggy*
8. **b)** *Lancia Beta Coupe*
9. **c)** *Big Stig*
10. **a)** *In a lavishly furnished apartment behind the Top Gear studio.*

Scores

8-10: *Start choosing a colour for your suit.*
4-7: *Lust for speed doesn't just happen, you have to work at it. Keep trying.*
0-3: *Oh dear. You're much more comfortable in normal clothes, aren't you?*

Race On!

As long as it's not James in the driver's seat, the lads have proven themselves to be more than capable when a race is on. From greyhounds to all-terrain skateboarders, the competitors have been a mixed bunch. How many can you remember?

1. Snooker player Ronnie O'Sullivan managed to pot 15 balls before The Stig could drive a full lap of the test track in what make of car?

a) Mercedes SL500
b) Bugatti Veyron
c) Porsche Carrera GT
d) Jaguar XK-R

2. James raced a Ford SportKa against what type of animal – and lost dismally?

a) Jaguar
b) Greyhound
c) Thoroughbred racehorse
d) Racing pigeon

3. Not surprisingly, James was again beaten by a professional bobsleigh team in which European country?

a) Switzerland
b) France
c) Iceland
d) Norway

How **hard** can it be?

4. Which Scandinavian city was the destination in a race between Jeremy in a Mercedes SLR McLaren and James and Richard travelling by plane, ferry and speedboat?

a) Oslo
b) Copenhagen
c) Stockholm
d) Reykjavik

5. In a race to determine the fastest way to travel across London, which form of transport came out on top?

a) Powerboat
b) Bicycle
c) Mercedes GL 500
d) Public transport

6. James was beaten in what make of car, by a group of BMX cyclists in Budapest?

a) Ascari A10
b) Mini Clubman
c) Fiat Nuova 500
d) Audi RS4

7. Not even a change of scenery could improve James' fortunes. He was soundly beaten by a downhill mountain biker in which European city?

a) Barcelona
b) Madrid
c) Lisbon
d) Paris

8. The best way to beat a Mitsubishi Lancer Evo Group N rally car in a race on a muddy downhill course in Wales, is to use one of these...

a) Hanglider
b) Grass skis
c) All-terrain skateboard
d) Mountain bike

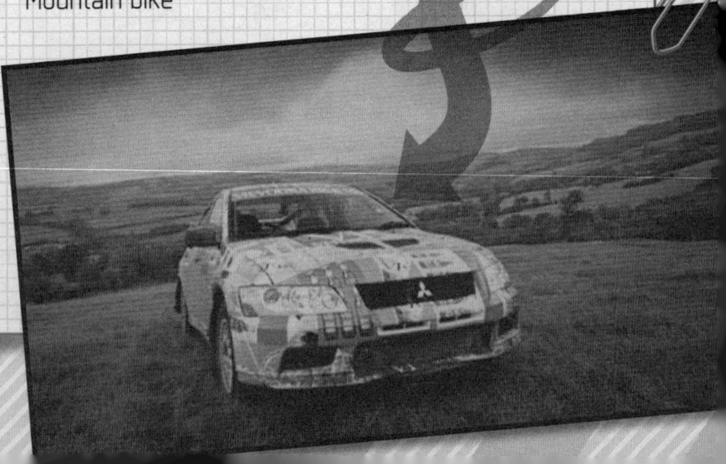

9. Richard took a turn at racing against an animal. His attempt, in a zippy MX-5, proved unsuccessful. What beat him?

a) Jaguar
b) Greyhound
c) Thoroughbred racehorse
d) Racing pigeon

10. And in order to beat a German on rollerskates, wearing a rocket jetpack on his back, you ought to consider driving one of these...

a) Aston Martin V8 Vantage
b) Ferrari 599 GTB Fiorano
c) Alfa Romeo 159
d) Mitsubishi Evo X

Answers

1. a) Mercedes SL500
2. d) Racing pigeon
3. d) Norway
4. a) Oslo
5. b) Bicycle
6. c) Fiat Nuova 500
7. c) Lisbon
8. c) All-terrain skateboard
9. b) Greyhound
10. a) Aston Martin V8 Vantage

Scores

8-10: You're like a greyhound on an all-terrain skateboard racing James through the back streets of Lisbon. Unstoppable!

4-7: C'mon, you know how to ride a bike, don't you?

0-3: Maybe you should take up sailing...

Who Said That? Part I

Actions speak louder than words. But sometimes the stuff that comes out of the lads' mouths simply can't be topped. Who said the following? Was it Jeremy, James or Richard?

1. "I am a driving God!"
   JEREMY JAMES RICHARD
2. "I am an alien!"
   JEREMY JAMES RICHARD
3. "Some say that he appears on high value stamps in Sweden, and that he can catch fish with his tongue..."
   JEREMY JAMES RICHARD
4. "Stop interfering, you piece of... cheap electronic tat!"
   JEREMY JAMES RICHARD

5. "The only thing I keep in my car is a little paintbrush for cleaning dust out of the switches."

JEREMY JAMES RICHARD

6. "It's no wonder Michael Schumacher retired, he's slower than me!"

JEREMY JAMES RICHARD

7. "I am not peeling a squirrel!"

JEREMY JAMES RICHARD

8. "I could say 'Maserati' before I could say 'Mummy'!"

JEREMY JAMES RICHARD

9. "Float! OLIVER!"

JEREMY JAMES RICHARD

10. "That is the delicate sound of thunder."

JEREMY
JAMES
RICHARD

Answers

1. Richard
2. Jeremy
3. Jeremy
4. James
5. James
6. James
7. Richard
8. Jeremy
9. Richard
10. Jeremy

Scores

8-10: After that brilliant score, there's nothing left to say.

4-7: So you're more interested in the cars, are you? Pay attention!

0-3: It's simple. Jeremy is the tall one, Richard's the short one and James has the bad hair.

The USA Road Trip Challenge

True or False

The land of the brave and the home of the free. Jeremy, James and Richard met all sorts of colourful characters on their US trek. It wouldn't be a *Top Gear* challenge without a little excitement now, would it? Test your knowledge of the USA Road Trip Challenge.

1. The lads' journey would take them from San Francisco to New Orleans.
   TRUE / FALSE

2. They first had to buy a used American car for no more than $1,000.
   TRUE / FALSE

3. The Stig's American counterpart was dubbed 'Fat Stig'.
   TRUE / FALSE

CHUG CHUGGA BRRRMMM

4. Richard's Dodge Pick-up was the slowest around the Moroso Motorsports Park.

TRUE / FALSE

5. Challenge No. 2 was was a braking test. Each of the cars had to get to 50mph and then stop before reaching a river filled with crocodiles.

TRUE / FALSE

6. One evening Jeremy went out to look for dinner and came back with a whole dead cow.

TRUE / FALSE

7. Richard painted 'Country and western is rubbish' on Jeremy's car.

TRUE / FALSE

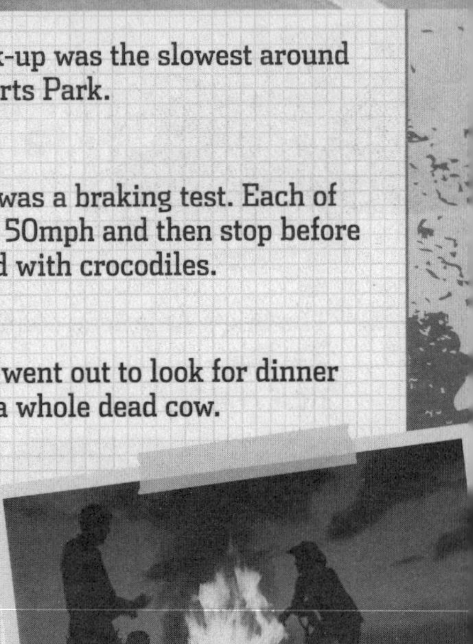

8. The Governor of Alabama ordered local police to escort the team out of the state.

TRUE / FALSE

9. In New Orleans, the team were shocked by the devastation caused by Hurricane Bertha.

TRUE / FALSE

10. Surprisingly, Jeremy was declared the loser, as he was unable to give his car away.

TRUE / FALSE

Answers

1. False. Miami to New Orleans.
2. True
3. False. Though rather tubby, he was called 'Big Stig'.
4. True
5. False. The river was filled with alligators.
6. True
7. True
8. False. Locals convinced the team it was time to leave.
9. False. The devastation was caused by Hurricane Katrina.
10. False. James was the one who failed to find an interested motorist.

Scores

8-10: Like totally awesome score dude!

4-7: It's okay, there's some bits from this challenge you probably wanted to forget anyway. Like the cow tied to Jeremy's roof!

0-3: Did the thunderstorm wash your care for Top Gear away?

Cool Wall Odd One Out Part 2

Any luck last time? Well, don't give up. If you want to be on top of the latest and greatest machines on four wheels (never two!), you have to know what you're talking about. Agreeing with Jeremy wouldn't hurt either.

1. Vauxhall Agila, Jaguar X-Type, Citroën C-Crosser, Seat Toledo

2. Volvo XC90, Subaru Impreza, Peugeot 308, Renault Clio
3. Fiat Doblo, Fiat 500, Subaru B9 Tribeca, Vauxhall Vectra
4. Land Rover Defender, Volvo S40, Mercedes C-Class, BMW 3-Series

5. Land Rover Discovery, Jeep Wrangler, Nissan Pathfinder, Land Rover Freelander

6. Subaru Impreza, Skoda Superb, Peugeot 1007, Kia Sportage

7. Toyota Landcruiser, Kia Sportage, Subaru Forester, BMW X3

8. Porsche Cayenne, Audi Q7, Volvo S60, Vauxhall Signum

9. Skoda Roomster, Fiat Panda, Suzuki Swift, Honda FR-V

10. Ferrari 308 GT4, Ferrari F40, Ferrari 599 GTB, Ferrari 512BB

Answers

1. **Citroën C-Crosser** (Uncool, the others are Seriously Uncool)
2. **Volvo XC90** (Uncool, the others are Cool)
3. **Fiat 500** (Sub-Zero, the others are Seriously Uncool)
4. **Land Rover Defender** (Sub-Zero, the others are Uncool)
5. **Jeep Wrangler** (Seriously Uncool, the others are Cool)
6. **Subaru Impreza** (Cool, the others are Uncool)
7. **Subaru Forester** (Cool, the others are Uncool)
8. **Volvo S60** (Cool, the others are Seriously Uncool)
9. **Skoda Roomster** (Seriously Uncool, the others are Cool)
10. **Ferrari 599 GTB** (Cool, the others are Uncool)

Scores

8-10: *Hey Jeremy, we know it's you!*
4-7: *Oh well. Everyone has different tastes.*
0-3: *Stick to walking.*

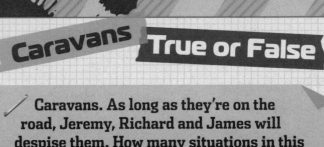

Caravans True or False

Caravans. As long as they're on the road, Jeremy, Richard and James will despise them. How many situations in this collection of classic caravan carnage can you recall?

1. A Volvo 240, at top speed, can jump over three caravans.
   TRUE / FALSE

2. And a stretch limousine will successfully jump over a wedding party without damaging a single caravan.
   TRUE / FALSE

3. In the destructive sport of Motorhome Racing, competitors must drive around a race track at high speed, towing a motorhome.
   TRUE / FALSE

4. On a caravan holiday in Dorset, Richard and *Top Gear* Dog were kidnapped by an elderly female fan.
TRUE / FALSE

5. Jeremy accidentally destroyed his caravan, burning it down while trying to cook chips.
TRUE / FALSE

6. After the caravan holiday film, the team received 70 complaints.
TRUE / FALSE

7. Richard and James played a game of conkers using six caravans.
TRUE / FALSE

8. Even though they placed a caravan over the bullseye, neither Richard or James managed to hit the top score in a game of car darts.

TRUE / FALSE

9. The fastest way to burn a caravan is to use the jet exhaust of a drag racer.

TRUE / FALSE

10. James broke the land speed record for a caravan when he towed it behind a Mitsubishi Evo 7.

TRUE / FALSE

Answers

1. False. It can make it over two (just).
2. Obviously false. The limo managed to get over the outdoor setting but completely totalled one of the caravans.
3. False. The motorhome is an all-in-one caravan and car.
4. True
5. True
6. False. They received 150!
7. True
8. False. Richard hit the bullseye on his final 'throw'. And, of course, the caravan was destroyed.
9. True
10. False. He failed and so destroyed the caravan by dropping it from a crane.

Scores

8-10: *C'mon, they're just innocent caravans! Why do you hate them so much?*

4-7: *Admit it. You have a soft spot for the happy little holiday homes.*

0-3: *Get out of the way, slow coach!*

Who Said That? Part 2

If the lads continue pulling out these gems, you'll start hearing them in the street. Or maybe not...

1. "This is a car programme. There will be no cushions, there will be no rag-rolling, no-one will sing, and at the end of the series, no one will have a recording contract."

   JEREMY JAMES RICHARD

2. "I've won something on *Top Gear*!"

   JEREMY JAMES RICHARD

3. "Atom heart mother!"

   JEREMY JAMES RICHARD

4. "We are grown men playing conkers with caravans."

JEREMY JAMES RICHARD

5. "A bit of cheese with that would be delicious."

JEREMY
JAMES
RICHARD

6. "This is a road car, and I'm up to 404... 405, come on!"

JEREMY JAMES RICHARD

7. "How hard can it be to build a kit car?"

JEREMY JAMES RICHARD

8. "I don't wanna be upside down!"

JEREMY JAMES RICHARD

9. "He's wearing cowboy boots!"

JEREMY
JAMES
RICHARD

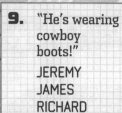

10. "Breaker Breaker One-Nine Contact Eyeball Ten Ten 'till we do it again Captain Slow."

JEREMY JAMES RICHARD

Answers

1. Jeremy
2. James
3. Jeremy
4. Richard
5. Jeremy
6. James
7. James
8. Richard
9. Jeremy
10. James

Scores

8-10: Considered a career as a Top Gear presenter?

4-7: If you've made it this far, you must really love Top Gear.

0-3: Whaddya want? A list of answers?

Chronicles of Captain Slow

True or False

What can be said about the man with an encyclopedic knowledge of all things car-related? Quite a bit actually. Learn more about the hair with the human attached below. That is, of course, if you can sort the true statements from the fakes.

1. Set the challenge of building an amphibious vehicle, James put a sail on a Triumph Herald. It sank immediately.

   TRUE / FALSE

2. On his second attempt to cross the Channel, James added a centreboard keel that enabled his Triumph Herald to sail properly.

   TRUE / FALSE

I'm going to fit it with a mast and some sails. **How brilliant is that?**

3. Though his nickname is Captain Slow, James' one strength on the road is navigating.

TRUE / FALSE

4. He is a qualified light aircraft pilot.

TRUE / FALSE

5. And he can play the piano and trombone.

TRUE / FALSE

6. On the American Challenge, James had 'NASCAR sucks' painted on the side of his car by Jeremy.

TRUE / FALSE

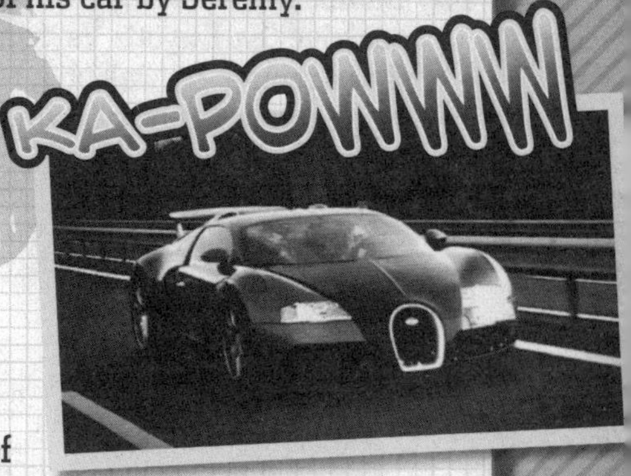

7. James was given the task of driving singer Lemar to the BRIT Awards, but got lost and never arrived.

TRUE / FALSE

8. Under the tutelage of racing legend Sir Jackie Stewart, Captain Slow managed to reduce his lap time of the Oulton Park circuit in a TVR Tuscan by 20 seconds.

TRUE / FALSE

9. In a race across Liverpool against two parkour enthusiasts (blokes who basically jump from building to building) James just manages to cross the finish line first in his Peugeot 207.

TRUE / FALSE

10. James had little luck when given the opportunity to drive the Bugatti Veyron at maximum speed. Even though he was on a test track, James couldn't quite reach the mark, blaming the wet road and high winds.

TRUE / FALSE

Answers

1. *False. This was one challenge James actually won.*
2. *False. Don't be ridiculous. It sank on the first attempt.*
3. *False. His sense of direction is even worse than his lap times.*
4. *True. Though, when we last checked he couldn't fly at night.*
5. *False. He plays the piano and flute.*
6. *True.*
7. *True. Poor Lemar.*
8. *True. Amazing but true.*
9. *False. Same old story – Captain Slow got lost.*
10. *False. For a brief time, Captain Slow was faster than anything else on the road.*

Scores

8-10: Well done! Do you have lustrous locks as well?

4-7: Like the Captain himself, a little slow off the mark.

0-3: I think you need to watch more Top Gear.

Stupidly Hard Quiz!

Yeah okay, the questions up to now haven't been all that easy, but you've reached this far, haven't you? Well then, these 20 Stupidly Hard Questions should be about as easy as controlling a Lotus Exige on a wet track. Get to it!

1. **Which female celebrity faced disqualification after failing to properly complete some corners?**

a) Billie Piper
b) Davina McCall
c) Joanna Lumley
d) Jodie Kidd

2. **What is *Top Gear*'s greatest ever driving song as voted by viewers?**

a) 'Danger Zone' by Kenny Loggins
b) 'I Should Be So Lucky' by Kylie Minogue
c) 'Get Ready To Wiggle' by The Wiggles
d) 'Don't Stop Me Now' by Queen

3. **Which singer broke the wheel off the Liana during his test drive?**

a) Trevor Eve
b) Jay Kay
c) Vinnie Jones
d) Lionel Richie

It's **quite** quick.

4. What car did Jeremy drive around the *Top Gear* test track until it ran out of petrol?

a) Koenigsegg CCX
b) Ford GT
c) Ascari A10
d) Volvo 240

5. What car did Jeremy dub 'an Enzo in drag'?

a) Ferrari Enzo
b) Pagani Zonda F
c) Aston Martin DBS
d) Maserati MC12

6. In a race against a Eurofighter Typhoon, Richard, driving a Bugatti Veyron, was beaten by how many seconds?

a) 2
b) 4
c) 7
d) 40

7. **As accompaniment to Richard's announcement that he was shipping 'Oliver' the Opel Kadett home to England, James played what tune on his portable keyboard?**

a) 'Canon in D' by Johann Pachelbel
b) 'Some Enchanted Evening' by Rodgers and Hammerstein
c) 'I Adore Mi Amor' by Color Me Badd
d) 'Romeo and Juliet Theme' by Nino Rota

8. **What was the nationality of the turbo-powered roller skater beaten by Richard in an Aston Martin V8 Vantage?**

a) Australian
b) Swiss
c) German
d) British

9. **How many motorcycles can a double-decker bus jump over?**

a) 2
b) 3
c) 7
d) 9

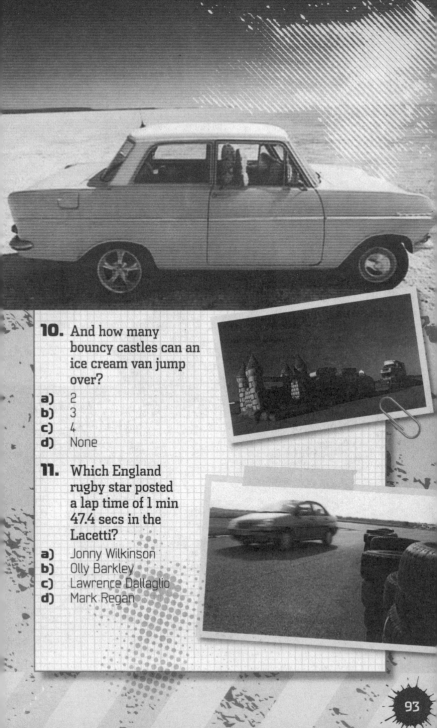

10. And how many bouncy castles can an ice cream van jump over?

a) 2
b) 3
c) 4
d) None

11. Which England rugby star posted a lap time of 1 min 47.4 secs in the Lacetti?

a) Jonny Wilkinson
b) Olly Barkley
c) Lawrence Dallaglio
d) Mark Regan

12. Which country launched its own version of *Top Gear* in 2008?

a) China
b) United States
c) Australia
d) France

13. What time did singer James Blunt post, on a suitably wet track?

a) 1 min 48.3 secs
b) 1 min 49 secs
c) 1 min 54.2 secs
d) Did not finish

14. Who is the fastest F1 star around the *Top Gear* test track?

a) Sebastian Vettel
b) Jenson Button
c) Lewis Hamilton
d) Damon Hill

15. Jeremy compared a real life lap in a Honda NSX with a lap he completed in which popular Playstation 2 game?

a) Grand Theft Auto
b) Super Tetris
c) Micro Machines 3
d) Gran Turismo 4

16. **What did Jeremy do his best to avoid on the British army's Salisbury Plain?**

a) Apache Attack Chopper
b) Austin-Healey Sprite
c) Challenger 2 Tank
d) Rocket-powered German on roller skates

17. **Which car took Car of the Year in 2006?**

a) Mercedes-Benz McLaren
b) Caterham 7 kit car
c) Lamborghini Gallardo Spyder
d) Subaru Legacy Outback

18. **And what won the year before?**

a) Bugatti Veyron
b) Volkswagen Golf
c) Aston Martin DB5
d) Ford GT

19. **Dame Ellen MacArthur set the fastest lap time of any celebrity in the Liana. What else is she known for?**

a) Speed skating
b) Sailing
c) Cooking
d) Acting

20. **Which car was the named the worst of 2007?**

a) Mini Clubman
b) Suzuki Swift
c) G-Wiz
d) Hyundai Accent

Answers coming up after this brief colourful interlude...

Supercar Parts

So you think you know your Ferrari from your Maserati? Take a close look at these supercars and see if you can guess the right model.

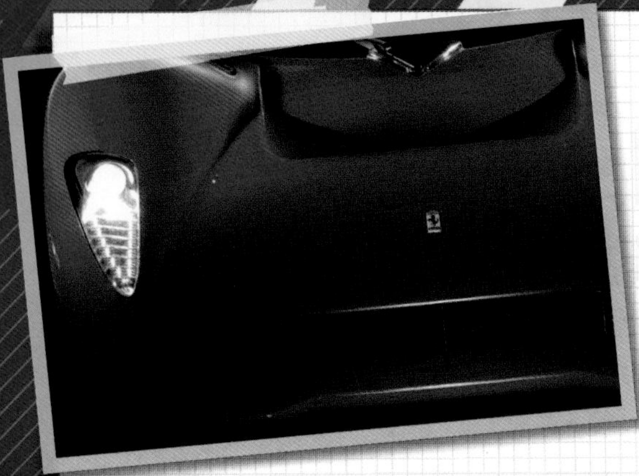

A. ______________________________

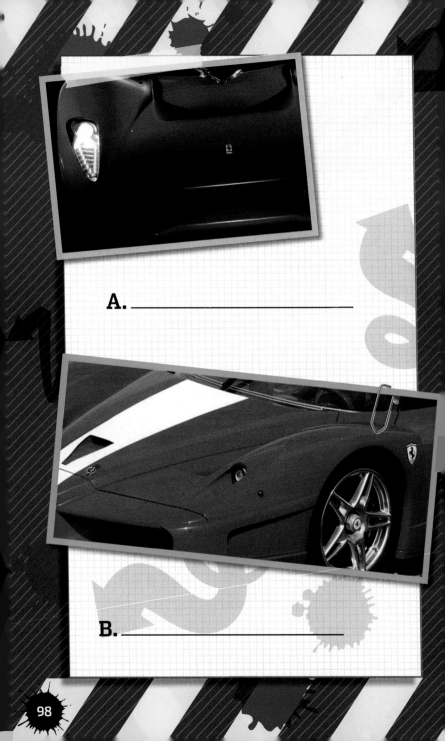

B. ______________________________

I don't think I'll **ever, ever** get out of it!

C. ______________________________

D. ______________________________

E. ______________________________

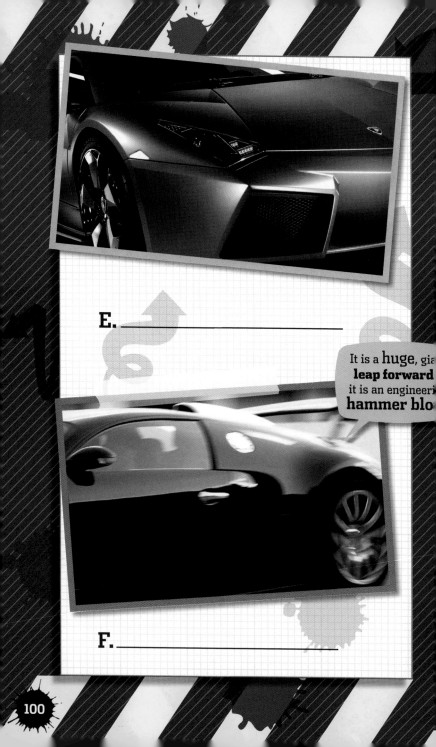

It is a huge, gia
leap forward
it is an engineeri
hammer blo

F. ______________________________

G. ______________________________

H. ______________________________

I. ______________________________

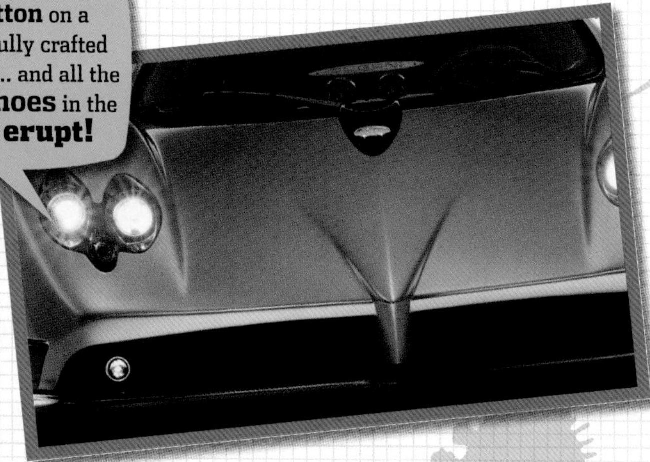
It's like pressing a **button** on a beautifully crafted **watch**... and all the **volcanoes** in the world **erupt!**

J. ______________________________

K. ______________________________

It's like putting a Saturn V **rocket** in a food blender!

L. ______________________________

Answers

A. Ferrari P4/5
B. Ferrari FXX
C. Ford GT
D. Lamborghini Reventon
E. Lamborghini Spyder
F. Bugatti Veyron
G. Maserati Granturismo
H. Koenigsegg CCX
I. Porsche 911 GT3
J. Pagani Zonda F
K. Aston Martin DBS
L. Lotus Exige S

WHOSE WHEELS?

Jeremy, Richard and James love a challenge, not least because they never know what kind of wheels they'll end up with. Take a look at these close-ups of various vehicles and see if you can identify whose is whose.

Amphibious cars Part 2 - the Channel

01 a:

01 b:

01 c:

Lightweight supercars in search of the perfect driving road

02 a:

02 b:

02 c:

British Leyland cars

03 a:

03 b:

03 c:

Lorrying

04 a:

04 b:

04 c:

Vietnam – the final leg

05 a:

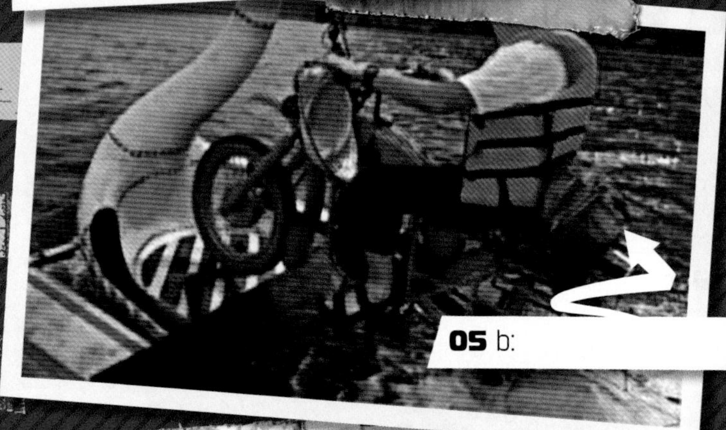

05 b:

05 c:

American muscle cars at Bonneville Salt Flats

06 a:

06 b:

06 c:

£1000 Alfa Romeos

07 a:

07 b:

07 c:

Answers

01 a: Richard
01 b: Jeremy
01 c: James
02 a: Richard
02 b: James
02 c: Jeremy
03 a: Jeremy
03 b: James
03 c: Richard
04 a: James
04 b: Jeremy
04 c: Richard
05 a: Jeremy
05 b: Richard
05 c: James
06 a: James
06 b: Richard
06 c: Jeremy
07 a: Richard
07 b: James
07 c: Jeremy

Answers

1. a) *Billie Piper*
2. d) *'Don't Stop Me Now' by Queen*
3. d) *Lionel Richie*
4. b) *Ford GT*
5. d) *Maserati MC12*
6. a) *2*
7. d) *'Romeo and Juliet Theme' by Nino Rota*
8. c) *German*
9. b) *3 (and crashed into eleven others)*
10. d) *None (Spectacular, but pathetic)*
11. c) *Lawrence Dallaglio*
12. c) *Australia*
13. a) *1 min 48.3 secs*
14. a) *Sebastian Vettel*
15. d) *Gran Turismo 4*
16. c) *Challenger 2 Tank*
17. c) *Lamborghini Gallardo Spyder*
18. a) *Bugatti Veyron*
19. b) *Sailing*
20. c) *G-Wiz*

Scores

15-20: *If a Porsche GT was the prize for top marks in this section, you'd win it. Unfortunately for you, there is no prize.*

7-14: *Considering these were the Stupidly Hard Questions, you should still be pleased with your score. Actually, on second thoughts, it was pretty rubbish.*

0-6: *Look on the bright side. You can always turn to the start of the book and do it all over again.*

5354 WWY 67
Veyron

WHICH Presenter Are You?

01 Which one of these cars would you choose to have in your garage?

a) Fiat Panda
b) Porsche 911
c) Lamborghini Gallardo Spyder

02 What is the most distinctive thing about your appearance?

a) Lustrous locks **b)** Very white teeth **c)** Very tall

03 If you were presented with an unusual challenge, what would you do?

a) Break out a piece of paper and draw some diagrams
b) Strap on a helmet and get stuck in
c) Say it's impossible but give it a go anyway

04 You're not very good at one thing. What is it?

a) Driving in the right direction
b) Reaching to the top of the Cool Wall
c) Admitting you're wrong

05 If you were to drive across London at peak time, what mode of transport would you use?

a) A Chelsea tractor
b) An expensive bicycle
c) A power boat

06 If you happened to accidentally break a £1 million car wash, what would you do?

a) Run
b) Run
c) Run

07 If you were to make your own police car, what would you do?

a) Fit an ice cream van speaker as a siren
b) Fit a self-deploying spike strip
c) Fit spikes on the wheels

08 What would you crash into if you were driving a lorry for a challenge?

a) Water cooler bottles
b) Demountable building
c) Brick wall

09 If you were to go on holiday to Vietnam, what sort of local cuisine would you like?

a) Snake meat
b) Nothing unusual
c) Pickled pig's ear

10 If you were to break a camera filming you, how would you do it?

a) Driving a super fast power boat through choppy waters
b) Sinking your amphibious car
c) Falling off a Vespa

Answers

Mostly as: *You're most like James. Slow and steady wins the race – but only if you keep going in the right direction.*

Mostly bs: *You're most like Richard. Willing to give anything a go and always keen to make up new kinds of sports. Like motorhome racing.*

Mostly cs: *You're most like Jeremy. Always right and gets very excited about supercars, so much so, you have driven one until it ran out of petrol.*

ARE YOU THE STIG?

Someone has to be The Stig. Could you be our tame racing driver? Check the statements below and then maybe the biggest problem bothering humankind will be answered.

01 Some say you only have one outfit.

TRUE/FALSE

02 Some say you only ever wear a helmet.

TRUE/FALSE

03 Some say you have taught stars to drive in Reasonably-Priced Cars.

TRUE/FALSE

STIG

04 Some say you sleep upside down.
TRUE/FALSE

05 Some say no one knows your true identity.
TRUE/FALSE

06 Some say you like to drive fast.
TRUE/FALSE

07 Some say you appear on a television show called Top Gear.
TRUE/FALSE

08 Some say you drive cars with immense talent and precision.
TRUE/FALSE

09 Some say you listen to morse code whilst driving.
TRUE/FALSE

10 Some say you can literally smell corners.
TRUE/FALSE

Answers

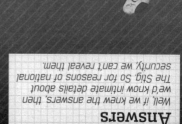

Well, if we knew the answers, then we'd know intimate details about The Stig. So for reasons of national security, we can't reveal them.

The Power Lap

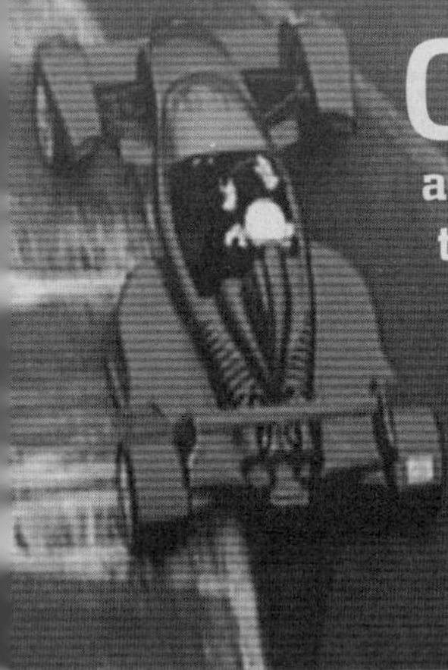

One of the most nail-biting parts of *Top Gear* is finding out where a supercar is going to be placed on the board. When will the top spot be knocked off? Will The Stig reveal more about himself and his driving? There's only one way to find out – answer these questions.

01 What is one of the attributes a car must have to qualify for a Power Lap?

a) Be very, very expensive
b) Have a stereo so The Stig can listen to morse code
c) Be able to go over a speed hump

02 What does The Stig do before each Power Lap?

a) Turn off the traction control
b) Turn up the stereo
c) Turn on the turbo charger

03 What is the fastest production car around the *Top Gear* track?

a) Ariel AtomV8 500
b) Gumpert Apollo Se
c) Bugatti Veyron 16.4

POWER LAP TIMES

04 What is the fastest supercar Power Lap time around the *Top Gear* track?

a) 1 minute 17.1 seconds
b) 1 minute 15.1 seconds
c) 1 minute 16.1 seconds

05 What is the slowest car to do a Power Lap?

a) Maserati 3200 GT
b) Porsche Pain Au Chocolat
c) Bowler Wildcat

06 What extra bit did the Koenigsegg CCX have added to it to make it go faster?

a) Racing formulated petrol
b) Extra power
c) Spoiler

07 Why didn't the Aston Martin DBR9 qualify to go on the Power Lap board?

a) It is a concept car
b) It wasn't road legal
c) The Stig didn't drive it

08 What happened to the Koenigsegg the first time The Stig drove it?

a) A tyre blew
b) It ran into the tyre wall
c) It broke down

09 Which presenter has had their own car driven by The Stig on a Power Lap?

a) James
b) Richard
c) Jeremy

10 What is the fastest Ferrari on the Power Lap board?

a) Enzo Ferrari
b) Ferrari 430 Scuderia
c) Ferrari 599 GTB Fiorano

VARROOOMMM

Answers

01 c) *The supercar must be completely roadworthy.*
02 a) *No traction control so The Stig can take control*
03 b) *Ariel Atom V8 500*
04 b) *1 minute 15.1 seconds*
05 b) *Porsche Pain Au Chocolat*
06 c) *The Top Gear spoiler gave it the extra speed it needed.*
07 b) *It was made for racing only, not as a road car.*
08 b) *The only time The Stig has ever hit anything.*
09 c) *Jeremy had his Mercedes-Benz SLS55 AMG driven.*
10 a) *Of course the Ferrari named after the owner of Ferrari should be fastest*

Scores

8-10: *You really, really like supercars, don't you?*
4-7: *You were too busy trying to figure out who The Stig is, weren't you?*
0-3: *Are caravanning holidays more your style?*

COOL WALL
Odd One Out Part 3

What are the rules of the Cool Wall? Well, it's not really about the car itself, it's more about how it makes the person look and feel when they're driving it. What will fellow motorists think? Be rendered speechless in awe, frozen solid in the radiating coolness, or laugh themselves stupid? Anyone's guess and it's something that Richard and Jeremy could argue on and on... and on about. Can you pick the odd one out in the lists of cars below?

01 Porsche Cayenne, Bentley Continental GT, Maserati Quattroporte

02 Bugatti Veyron, Ferrari Enzo, McLaren Mercedes SLR

03 Toyota Prius, Mini Cooper, Renault Laguna

04 Ford Mondeo, Aston Martin DBS, Porsche Cayman

05 Audi TT, VW Scirocco, Suzuki Liana

06 Dodge Viper, Rolls-Royce Phantom, Koenigsegg CCX

07 Fiat 500, Alfa Romeo 147, Citroën C2

08 Land Rover Discovery, Range Rover Sport, VW Touareg R50

09 Aston Martin V8 Vantage, Aston Martin DB9, Mercedes SL

Answers

01 *Maserati Quattroporte (Sub Zero, the others are Seriously Uncool).*
02 *Bugatti Veyron (Uncool, the others are Cool).*
03 *Toyota Prius (Sub Zero, the others are Cool).*
04 *Porsche Cayman (Seriously Uncool, the others are Uncool).*
05 *VW Scirocco (Sub Zero, the others are Uncool).*
06 *Koenigsegg CCX (Seriously Uncool, the others are Cool).*
07 *Fiat 500 (Sub Zero, the others are Cool).*
08 *VW Touareg R50 (Uncool, the others are Seriously Uncool).*
09 *Aston Martin DB9 (Sub Zero, the others are Uncool).*
10 *Ferrari F430 (Cool, the others are Uncool).*

Scores

8-10: *You need your own fridge you're that cool. Sub, sub zero.*
4-7: *You know when you're in the bath and it's at that not-so-nice temperature? It's called lukewarm. A bit like your score.*
0-3: *Oh dear. If you got one right, there's hope for you to be sub zero yet. Just try a little bit harder, okay?*

10 Ferrari F430, Morgan Aeromax, Dodge Challenger

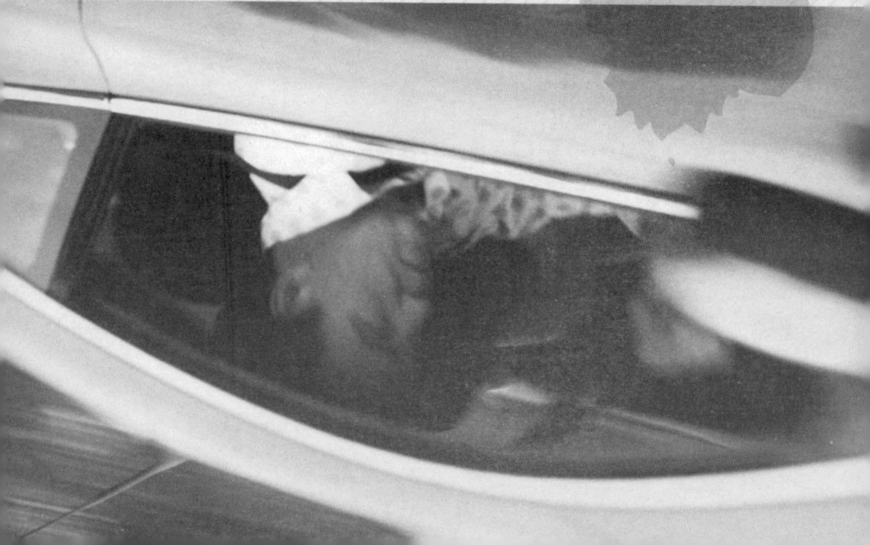

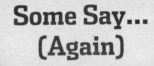

Some Say... (Again)

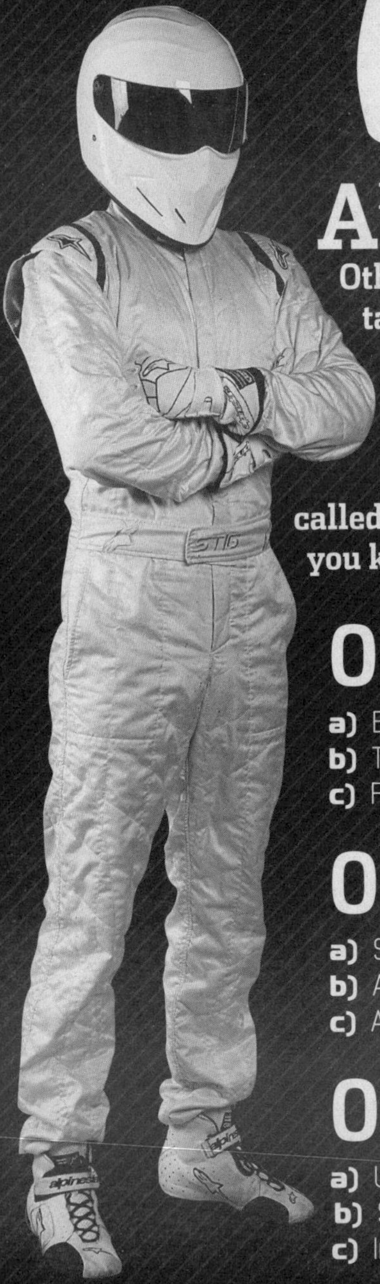

All we know about The Stig is rumour, myth, hearsay. Other than being *Top Gear*'s tame racing driver, he is an enigma wrapped in a mystery. Or a mystery wrapped in an enigma. All we do know is he is called The Stig. How much do you know about him?

01 Some say he is frightened of...

a) Bread
b) Trees
c) Flowers

02 Some say that it is impossibl for The Stig to wear...

a) Socks
b) Any other colour than white
c) A hat

03 Some say that he sleeps...

a) Upside down
b) Standing up
c) Inside out

04 Some say that he only eats...

a) Cheese
b) Leather
c) Boysenberry ice cream

05 Some say that if you lick his chest it tastes like...

a) Chocolate
b) Leather car seats
c) Piccalilli

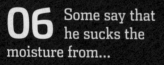

06 Some say that he sucks the moisture from...

a) Ducks
b) Wet hair
c) Wet dogs

07 Some say all his potted plants are called...

a) Barry
b) Steve
c) Stig

08 Some say that if you tune your radio to 88.4 you can...

a) Hear The Stig speak
b) Hear The Stig's thoughts
c) Hear The Stig sing

09 Some say that on really warm days he...

a) Sheds his skin like a snake
b) Takes his helmet off
c) Sweats petrol

10 Some say that his earwax tastes like...

a) Turkish delight
b) Gherkins
c) Strawberry jam

11 Some say that he was raised by...

a) Dogs **b)** Ducks **c)** Wolves

12 Some say he has an apartment...

a) In the Tower of London
b) At the top of the London Eye
c) In an Underground train

13 Some say his skin is the texture of...

a) Carbon fibre
b) Dolphins
c) Velour

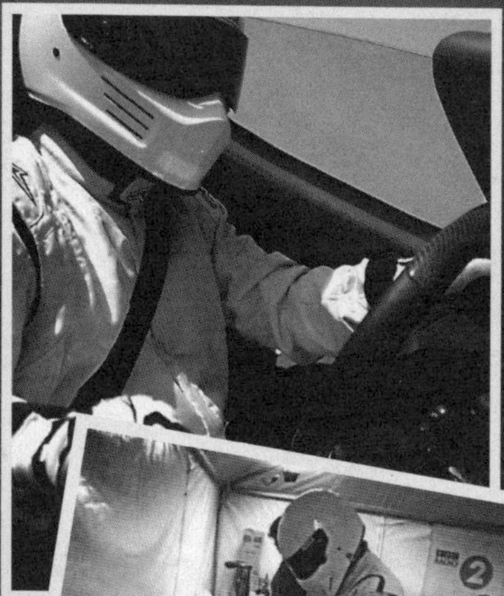

14 Some say he is wanted by...

a) The government of Botswana
b) The CIA
c) MI5

15 Some say his favourite food is...

a) Raw meat
b) Rubber
c) Raw fish

Answers

01 b) *Trees*
02 a) *Socks*
03 c) *Inside out*
04 a) *Cheese*
05 c) *Piccalilli*
06 a) *Ducks*
07 b) *Steve*
08 b) *Hear the Stig's thoughts*
09 a) *Sheds his skin like a snake*
10 a) *Turkish delight*
11 c) *Wolves*
12 b) *At the top of the London Eye*
13 b) *Dolphins*
14 b) *The CIA*
15 a) *Raw meat*

Scores

11-15: *Hang on, if you scored fifteen out of fifteen... is there something we should know? Are you The Stig?*

6-10: *You're good. You know many interesting facts about The Stig. This is very, very important information.*

0-5: *Do you know who The Stig is? Let's start with the basics – he's the tame racing driver.*

ALL ABOUT JEZZA

He's big. He's loud. He likes cars. And of course he's never wrong. So how well do you know Jeremy? Take the quiz below to see if you're just like Jeremy and never, ever wrong.

01 What kind of car did Jeremy once drive into a swimming pool?

a) Bentley **b)** Rolls-Royce **c)** Lincoln limousine

02 What was the name of the amphibious car that Jeremy crossed the English Channel in?

a) Suboatu
b) Toyboata
c) Nissank

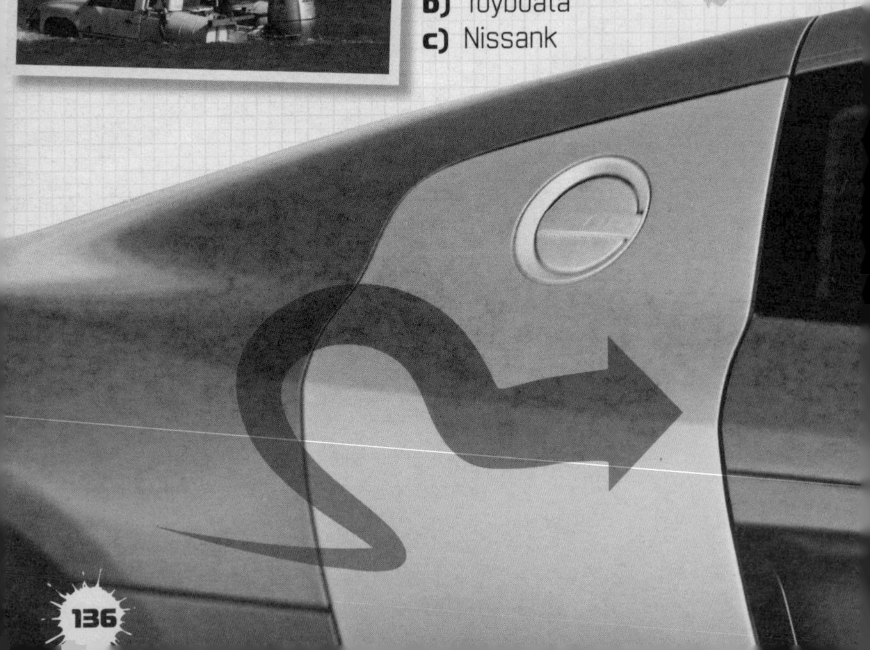

03 For the HGV challenge Jeremy had to do a hill start with something very precious belonging to him parked behind his lorry. What was it?

a) Drum kit
b) Framed autograph of Keira Knightley
c) Ford GT

04 Jeremy thoroughly enjoys conducting useful experiments on new gadgets. Once he attached a V8 engine to what?

a) Rocking chair
b) Food blender
c) Lawn mower

05 In the Make a Better Police Car Challenge, what modification did Jeremy make to his police car?

a) Added wheel covers with spikes
b) Added a periscope
c) Added ten different sounding sirens

06 Jeremy has a few favourite cars. Which of these is one of them?

a) Ferrari 430 Scuderia
b) Lamborghini Gallardo Spyder
c) Mercedes CLK63 AMG The Black Series

07 When Jeremy had to drive a Nissan GT-R through Japan in a race against Richard and James, what happened to his satnav?

a) He turned it off and took a long time to make it work again
b) He accidentally changed the language to German
c) He refused to listen to it and made his own way there

08 When the *Top Gear* team went on a search for the best driving road in the world, what car did Jeremy drive?

a) Bugatti Veyron
b) Lamborghini Gallardo Superleggera
c) Lamborghini Murcielago LP640

09 What did Jeremy do when he drove the Peel P50 to the BBC Centre?

a) Couldn't get the car into the lift so he had to abandon it
b) Crashed into the reception desk
c) Drove it through the News 24 studio when they were on air

10 What animal did Jeremy strap to the roof of his car in the Miami to New Orleans challenge?

a) A pig
b) A cow
c) A sheep

11 What happened when Jeremy tried to catch The Stig in his police car?

a) Jeremy smashed The Stig's windscreen
b) Jeremy's wheel fell off
c) Jeremy burnt out his gear box

12 What car did Jeremy decide to use to make his stretch limousine?

a) Ford Focus **b)** Fiat Panda **c)** Datsun 120Y

13 What was Jeremy cooking when he set the caravan on fire?

a) Bacon **b)** Chips **c)** Fish

14 Jeremy had the fastest tractor in the Grow Your Own Petrol Challenge. How fast did it go around the test track?

a) 2 minutes 30 seconds
b) 2 minutes 57 seconds
c) 3 minutes 12 seconds

15 When training for the Polar Challenge, what did Jeremy have to do?

a) Learn how to cook with one gas burner
b) Snowboard down a ski run
c) Jump into icy water

Answers

01 b) *Jeremy opened a public pool by driving a Rolls into it.*
02 c) *James and Richard hitched a ride as well.*
03 a) *He didn't hit his drum kit though. James and Richard did – with their bare hands.*
04 a) and b) *The gadgets didn't quite work – the rocking chair fell to pieces, and the blender didn't mash up the bricks very much.*
05 a) *The spikes looked pretty scary.*
06 c) *Jeremy declared the CLK63 as his favourite car.*
07 a) *Jeremy had panic in his eyes when he couldn't turn it back on.*
08 b) *Jeremy loves his Lambo.*
09 c) *The Peel P50 drove through the back of the studio.*
10 b) *Somehow he managed to get a cow onto the roof.*
11 b) *Jeremy's wheel fell off.*
12 b) *Jeremy's Fiat later broke in half.*
13 b) *The oil caught on fire.*
14 b) *So Jeremy lost the challenge.*
15 c) *Jeremy was shocked speechless when he was pushed into icy water.*

Scores

11-15: *Excellent! You are just like Jeremy! Always right!*
6-10: *Seems like sometimes you're too distracted by the cars to pay close enough attention.*
0-5: *Oh dear. Do you put your fingers in your ears when Jeremy speaks?*

SUPERCARS

How well do you know your Ferraris from your Lamborghinis? Your Aston Martins from your Bugattis? One thing we all know is that these cars are supercharged, super quick and super loud. Test your supercar knowledge with the questions below.

01 The Ferrari 599 has some pretty cool gadgets, for example, the steering wheel lights up to tell you when to change gear. **TRUE / FALSE**

02 In the time that it takes a Ford Mondeo to get from 0-60mph, the Ferrari 599 can get from 0-200mph. **TRUE / FALSE**

03 The Ascari A10 once had the fastest Power Lap time, but was knocked off the top spot by the Gumpert Apollo. **TRUE / FALSE**

04 The Bugatti Veyron is one of the fastest production cars in the world with a top speed of 253mph. **TRUE / FALSE**

05 The Ascari A10 goes back to the basics with a sequential gearbox – none of this flappy paddle transmission nonsense. **TRUE / FALSE**

06 Jeremy road tested the Porsche 911 GT2 against the Lamborghini Gallardo LP560-4 and thought the Porsche was definitely the best. **TRUE / FALSE**

07 The Pagani Zonda F Roadster has a completely naked carbon fibre body. **TRUE/FALSE**

08 In a drag race between a Bugatti Veyron and a Pagani Zonda F Roadster, the Bugatti won by a mile. **TRUE/FALSE**

09 One of the differences between the Aston Martin DBS and the Aston Martin DB9 is that the DBS has a carbon fibre body. **TRUE/FALSE**

10 When Jeremy test drove the Koenigsegg CCX on the test track, he reached 242mph and then needed a little lie down. **TRUE/FALSE**

11 In the drag race between the Porsche 911GT2 and the Lamborghini Gallardo LP560-4, the Porsche won. **TRUE/FALSE**

12 The Veritas RS III is built in a small factory in Somerset. **TRUE/FALSE**

13 In a test for fuel economy with supercars, the first supercar to run out of petrol was the Aston Martin DBS. **TRUE/FALSE**

14 In a drag race between the Lotus Elise and a Tesla Roadster, the Tesla won, much to Jeremy's disbelief.

TRUE/FALSE

15 The only car The Stig has hit the tyre wall with is a Koenigsegg CCX.

TRUE/FALSE

Answers

01 True

02 **False**. *The Ferrari 599 can get from 0-150mph in the same time as a Ford Mondeo gets from 0-60mph.*

03 **False**. *The Ascari A10 has 625bhp. Not quite enough to beat the Ferrari Enzo.*

04 **True**. *The F1 cars can only do 240mph.*

05 **True**. *Jeremy loved the sequential gearbox and really put the Ascari through its paces.*

06 **False**. *Jeremy screamed with fear when driving the Porsche.*

07 **True**. *James thinks it looks a bit silly but it makes the car solid which is what you want.*

08 **True**. *The Bugatti can reach 0-60mph a whole second faster than the Zonda.*

09 **True**. *But that didn't mean Jeremy liked it that much.*

10 **False**. *Jeremy reached 193mph and was speechless for a moment when he stopped.*

11 **False**. *The Porsche and the Lambo tied.*

12 **False**. *It is built in Germany.*

13 **False**. *The first to run out was the Ferrari 599.*

14 **True**. *But the Tesla later failed further Top Gear tests.*

15 **True**. *The Stig doesn't talk about it.*

Scores

11-15: *Power! You and The Stig might like to spend some time together doing a Power Lap or two.*

6-10: *You're heading in the right direction, but would still prefer a country drive with Captain Slow.*

0-5: *Now something tells me that caravans are more your style?*

ALL ABOUT THE HAMSTER

Richard. He's small. He's got white teeth. He likes cars. And of course he'll try pretty much anything once. So how well do you know Richard?

01 Richard is very passionate about the Cool Wall. He even ate one of the car cards rather than let Jeremy get his own way. What car did he eat?

a) Porsche 911 **b)** Aston Martin DB9 **c)** BMW M6

02 When trying out the new motorhome racing sport, Richard ran into a problem with his motorhome. What was it?

a) The accelerator got stuck
b) It completely disintegrated
c) It overheated and stopped working

03 When Richard went to Tokyo city to test drive the iReal, what did he discover?

a) It was a chair **b)** It was a scooter **c)** It was a unicycle

04 Richard's research was very thorough when he was investigating what bus would be best for London. How did he conduct his test?

a) Using the *Top Gear* team as drivers
b) Using touring car drivers
c) Using bus drivers

05 When Richard controversially decided all Aston Martins should be moved to 'Uncool' on the Cool Wall, what did Jeremy do?

a) Removed Richard's microphone
b) Shoved all the Aston Martin cards down his trousers
c) Put all the Aston cards where Richard couldn't reach them

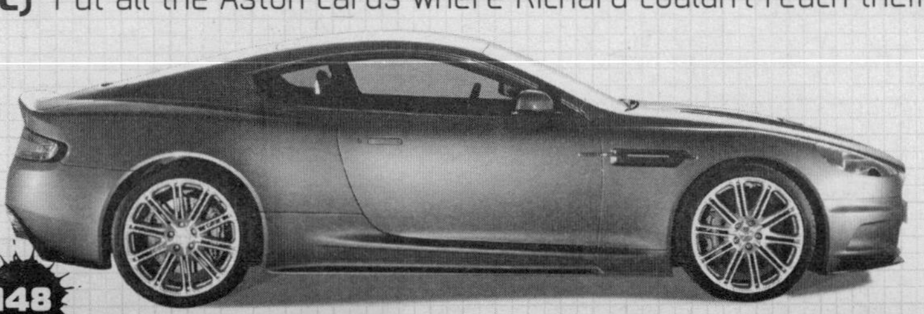

06

A new form of hunting invented involved chasing Jeremy in a Japanese off-road car, but what happened to Richard on his horse?

a) His horse bolted on him
b) He couldn't jump a fence
c) He lost the hunt

07

Which of these cars did the manufacturer refuse to lend Richard?

a) Ford Focus
b) Dodge Charger
c) Bugatti Veyron

08

When attempting to cross the Channel in his amphibious car, what problem did Richard encounter?

a) He wasn't tall enough to see properly when steering
b) His Dampervan immediately sank when it entered the water
c) His anchor fell off and got stuck

09 What car did Richard choose to drive during the Miami to New Orleans challenge?

a) Corvette **b)** Trans-Am **c)** Pick-up

10 To prove how easy F1 racing could be, Richard took an F1 car for a spin at Silverstone. It wasn't as easy as it looked though. What happened?

a) He stalled the engine eight times
b) He spun off the track eight times
c) His feet couldn't touch the pedals

11 What kind of car did Richard buy to turn into a police car?

a) Fiat Panda **b)** Suzuki Vitara **c)** Mini Cooper

12 What sort of modification did Richard make for his police car?

a) Added at least twenty flashing lights
b) Painted it black so it could be stealthy
c) Added a turbocharger to the engine

13 What did Richard do with the results of the Police Car Challenge?

a) Ate them
b) Set them alight
c) Hid them in the studio

14 What colour was Richard's motorcycle painted when they were in Vietnam?

a) Yellow
b) Pink
c) Red

15 Richard fell deeply in love with the Ferrari Daytona and he got a bad case of verbal diarrhoea. What stopped him?

a) The police pulled him over
b) He broke down
c) He started weeping tears of joy

Answers

01 c) *Jeremy thought it was Sub Zero and Richard vehemently disagreed.*
02 a) *There wasn't much left of Richard's motorhome when the race finished.*
03 a) *It was a chair. A very fancy one.*
04 b) *The touring car drivers weren't very gentle with the buses.*
05 a) *Richard was left shouting with no microphone.*
06 c) *Richard lost the hunt for a bit but soon found it again.*
07 b) *Richard owns a Dodge Charger.*
08 a) *Richard took a chance with not being able to see properly.*
09 c) *Richard loved his pick-up.*
10 a) *The car had to be taken back to the pit before Richard could try again.*
11 b) *Richard was teased mercilessly by James and Jeremy for his choice.*
12 a) *Richard looked like a mobile disco.*
13 a) *Richard ate them.*
14 b) *Richard wasn't very happy when his motorbike turned pink.*
15 a) *The police thought Richard had nicked the car.*

Scores

11-15: *You really are a fan of The Hamster. Do you whiten your teeth as well?*
6-10: *You might've been distracted by the cars, but try to pay attention to Richard as well, okay?*
0-5: *Richard is the short one with the artfully messy hair. He's a presenter on Top Gear.*

Who Said That?

Was it Jeremy, Richard or James?

Part 3

01 The acceleration is so **brutal** I feel like my eyes have been moved around the side of my head like a **pigeon's.**

02 Stop moving your **face** about with noises coming out of it. **Stop!**

03 I think we could forge a career as the world's **worst** explorers.

04 The **only** thing I keep in my car is a little paintbrush for cleaning **dust** out of the switches.

05 **Don't** hit it with a hammer!

This is Germany, there are **procedures** to go through... I **like** procedures.

06

07

I am **not** peeling a squirrel!

He looks like a **spaniel** that's crashed into the back of a **hen!**

08

09

It's **vicious** in an amusing way, like a **shark** wearing a funny hat.

10

Based on... **no** knowledge at all, we decided to **push on** in our three-ton truck.

Answers

01 James
02 Richard
03 Jeremy
04 James
05 James
06 James
07 Richard
08 Jeremy
09 Jeremy
10 Jeremy

Scores

8-10: Well done! You may one day become an official member of the Top Gear team.

4-7: So, did you only watch the Power Lap bits? Are you only interested in The Stig?

0-3: Did you know that there are three people on Top Gear called Jeremy, Richard and James?

POCKET ROCKETS

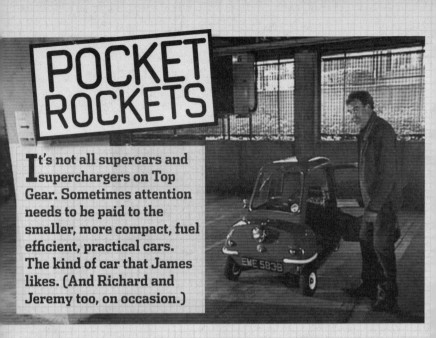

It's not all supercars and superchargers on Top Gear. Sometimes attention needs to be paid to the smaller, more compact, fuel efficient, practical cars. The kind of car that James likes. (And Richard and Jeremy too, on occasion.)

01 The Peel P50 is listed in the Guinness Book of Records as the smallest production car ever made. No wonder Jeremy had problems trying to fold himself, origami-style into the car. **TRUE/FALSE**

02 Jeremy didn't have any problems whizzing around the office in his Peel P50. Even going in and out of lifts was a doddle. **TRUE/FALSE**

03 Jeremy was curious to answer the eternal question – which is faster, a car or a man? So he jumped in a Nissan Micra and raced a marathon runner through rush hour. **TRUE/FALSE**

04 The world was turned upside down when it was proven that a man was indeed faster than a car through London rush-hour traffic. The marathon runner beat Jeremy by eleven minutes. **TRUE/FALSE**

05 The Volkswagen GTi W12 is one of the fastest selling cars in Volkswagen's history. Even Jeremy liked it. **TRUE/FALSE**

06 Jeremy thinks the Abarth 500 SS is a much, much better car than the Mini Cooper. He really believes that the Abarth Fiat 500 SS makes you feel happy. Tra la la. **TRUE/FALSE**

07 The top speed of the Abarth Fiat 500 SS is a surprisingly huge 142mph. **TRUE/FALSE**

08 The Golf GTi is made up of a mixed bag of parts from different car makes like Lamborghini, Bentley and Audi. **TRUE/FALSE**

09 When Richard met Oliver, it was love at first sight. This little Opel Kadett took Richard safely across 1,000 miles of Botswana with hardly any problems at all. **TRUE/FALSE**

10 When they were driving across the desert plains, the dust blowing in through the vents of Oliver was so bad, Richard had to wrap himself in scarves so his mouth wouldn't be full of grit.
TRUE/FALSE

Answers

01 True. *It took Jeremy a few attempts to get into the car.*

02 False. *There's no reverse gear in the Peel P50.*

03 False. *Jeremy drove a Fiat Panda.*

04 True. *Jeremy was absolutely gob-smacked.*

05 False. *The GTi W12 is a concept car that hasn't gone into production.*

06 True. *Jeremy was really taken with the Fiat 500 from Abarth.*

07 False. *The top speed is 131mph from its 180bhp engine.*

08 True. *Various bits and pieces from the three makes are put into a Volkswagen Golf.*

09 True. *Richard loves Oliver so much he brought him back to England.*

10 False. *Richard was smug and happy with no grit in his teeth. Unlike James and Jeremy.*

Scores

8-10: *You're a big fan of the Fiat Panda as well? You should go out for a Sunday drive with Captain Slow for some fun.*

4-7: *You're not quite convinced by the term 'Pocket Rocket'. You hear 'pocket rocket' and think 'small car'.*

0-3: *So, you're a supercars only sort of person, are you? Good things do come in small packages, you know, just ask Richard.*

VIETNAM SPECIAL PART 1

1,000 miles to travel. On two wheels. On 4 horsepower motorbikes. In Vietnam. Doesn't sound much like *Top Gear*, does it? But, much to Jeremy's horror, it is. How were they going to fare in some of the maddest traffic in the world? And was it going to be fun? Let's see...

01 The first challenge Jeremy, Richard and James were given was to buy some wheels. But with how much money?

a) 15 million dong
b) 25 million dong
c) 2 million dong

02 Jeremy was not too pleased that the money they received was only going to buy him 2 wheels instead of 4. What did he end up buying?

a) Honda Jazz 50
b) Gas Gas EC 50 Rookie
c) Lime green scooter

03 When Jeremy, Richard and James went to buy helmets they ran into some trouble. What was it?

a) Jeremy wanted to buy full safety gear but they didn't have any in his size
b) They were mobbed by *Top Gear* fans in the street
c) James' and Jeremy's heads were too large to fit any helmets in the shop

04 Once they were all on their way, Jeremy immediately ran into trouble with his little scooter and had to get a new engine. What did he say when it was fixed?

a) 'In no time at all, I will be overtaking James and Richard. Yes! I will win!'
b) 'Got a new engine, got a new gearbox. And it feels exactly the same!'
c) 'I hate this scooter. Who ever thought two wheels were a good idea?'

05 James and Jeremy love nothing more than playing practical jokes on Richard. What did they do to him?

a) Spray paint his bike with love hearts
b) Safety test his helmet by running over it with a lorry
c) Hide prawns in his bag so he would smell

06 As their bikes kept on running into problems, the *Top Gear* team were presented with a back-up vehicle that they would have to use if they broke down again. What was it?

a) Volkswagen Beetle
b) A motorcycle decorated with the American flag
c) An electric-powered bicycle

07 Jeremy was very kind to Richard and bought him a present that would always remind Richard of this journey. What was it?

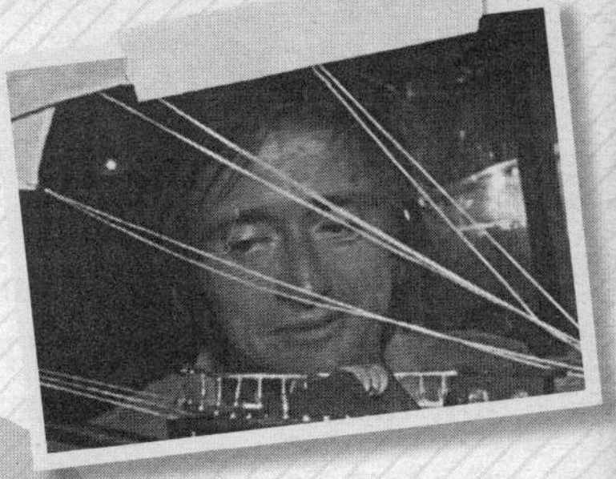

a) A giant model of a wooden sailing ship
b) A model of a motorcycle made out of tin
c) A model of an ancient ruin they visited

08 Jeremy couldn't wait to continue the goodwill and buy James a present. So Richard and Jeremy thought long and hard and bought him... what?

a) A traditional Vietnamese stone lion
b) A classical stone sculpture of a centaur
c) A classical stone sculpture of a pretty lady

09 Richard and James decided to take their bikes for a spin down the beach so Jeremy went and did what he knows how to do best. What was it?

a) Have a relaxing foot massage at the hotel
b) Go for a relaxing taxi ride in a 4-wheeled vehicle because he missed them so much
c) Planned what the next practical joke on Richard could be

10 Richard was a little bi careless when he was riding with his present on the back. What happened?

a) It knocked the statue off the back of James' bike
b) It knocked the side of a bin and a big bit fell off
c) It knocked a streetlight and came off the back of the bike

Answers

01 a) *And that did seem like quite a lot of money.*
02 c) *Richard and James thought Jeremy's choice wasn't the wisest. He'd soon learn.*
03 c) *Jeremy and James had to have custom helmets made.*
04 b) *There was no improvement for Jeremy and he wasn't happy about it.*
05 b) *Richard's replacement helmet was a pretty pastel pink.*
06 b) *This made Jeremy, James and Richard pray that their bikes would make it through.*
07 a) *Richard had to strap it to the back of his motorcycle and take it with him.*
08 c) *James seemed pretty touched by the fact that they actually thought about the present just a little bit.*
09 a) *After all the bumpy riding on the scooter he treated himself to a foot massage.*
10 b) *Richard drove with the mast dangling down the back of his bike.*

Scores

8-10: *Were you following the Top Gear team wearing a colander as a helmet?*
4-7: *So maybe you got up to make a cup of tea and missed out on some of the action?*
0-3: *Were you not watching Top Gear when this amazing special was on? You missed out.*

COOL WALL

Odd One Out Part 4

It's time for more of the Cool Wall. Make sure you know your Mercedes from your Aston Martins, and your Peugeots from your Pandas. Can you say which car is the odd one out in each group?

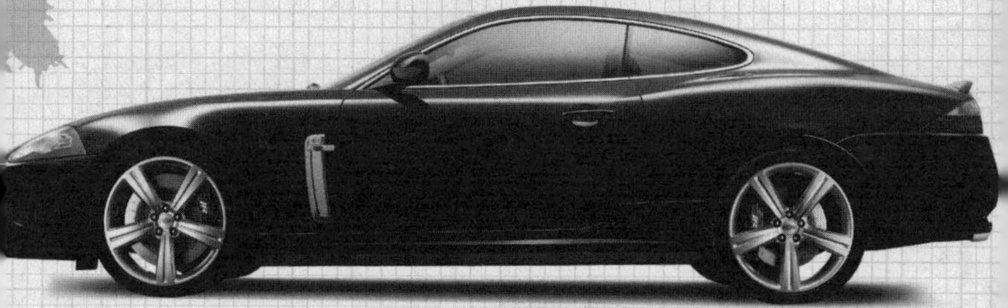

01 Aston Martin DB9, Jaguar XKR, BMW M3 Coupe

02 Jeep Cherokee, Hummer H1, Ford Galaxy

03 Alfa Romeo MiTo, Fiat 500 Abarth, Renault Clio

04 Mercedes CLS, Mini Clubman, Mazda 3

05 Mazda RX-8, Porsche 911 Cabriolet, VW Beetle Cabriolet

06 Morgan Aero 8, Chrysler Crossfire, Ferrari F430 Scuderia

07 Mazda MX5, VW Phaeton, Jaguar X Type

08 Jensen Interceptor S, PT Cruiser, Caterham 7

09 Porsche GT2, Porsche 91 GT3 RS, Nissan Micra Cabriolet

10 Mini Cabriolet, VW Scirocco, Daihatsu Copen

Answers

01 BMW M3 Coupe (Cool, the others are Sub Zero)
02 Hummer H1 (Seriously Uncool, the others are Uncool)
03 Fiat 500 Abarth (Sub Zero, the others are Cool)
04 Mercedes CLS (Cool, the others are Uncool)
05 Mazda RX-8 (Cool, the others are Seriously Uncool)
06 Morgan Aero 8 (Cool, the others are Uncool)
07 VW Phaeton (Sub Zero, the others are Cool)
08 Caterham 7 (Seriously Uncool, the others are Uncool)
09 Porsche GT2 (Uncool, the others are Seriously Uncool)
10 VW Scirocco (Sub Zero, the others are Cool)

Scores

8-10: *You need your own fridge you're that cool. Sub, sub zero.*

4-7: *You know when you're in the bath and it's at that not-so-nice temperature? It's called lukewarm. A bit like your score.*

0-3: *Oh dear. If you got one right, there's hope for you to be sub zero yet. Just try a little bit harder, okay?*

ALL ABOUT CAPTAIN SLOW

James. He's sensible. He's got big hair. He likes cars. And of course he'll draw you a diagram of just about anything technical. But how well do you know James?

01 What kind of modification did James make to his police car so he could catch crims?

a) Added a paint gun system
b) Added a detachable prison cell
c) Added a supersonic siren

02 How long did it take for James to start his tractor in the Grow Your Own Petrol challenge?

a) 1 hour
b) 5 minutes
c) 45 minutes

03 What was James' main problem with being at the North Pole?

a) He didn't want to be stuck in a car with Jeremy
b) He doesn't like snow
c) He doesn't like the outdoors

04 James loves his cars. Which of these does he own?

a) Porsche Boxster
b) Lamborghini Gallardo Spyder
c) Ferrari Daytona

05 What top speed did James get to in a Bugatti Veyron?

a) 260mph **b)** 253mph **c)** 214mph

06 What was the second supercar James got to power test?

a) Ascari A10
b) Pagani Zonda F Roadster
c) Gumpert Apollo

07 What did James say when he was power testing the supercar?

a) 'I'm giving it the beans!'
b) 'Oh, that didn't go well.'
c) 'Powerrrrrrrrr!'

08 What country did James visit to practise his driving for his supercar test?

a) Italy
b) Switzerland
c) Finland

09 What was the problem with James' amphibious car when he tried to cross the English Channel?

a) The rudder didn't work
b) It sank
c) The mast broke

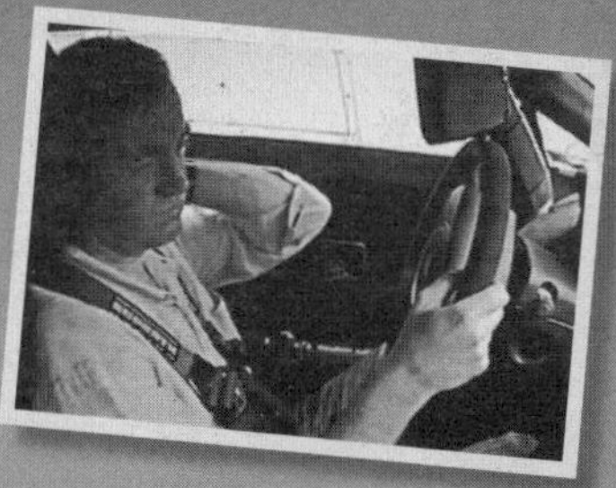

10 James chose an interesting car in the *Top Gear* quest for the perfect driving road in the world. What was his car?

a) Aston Martin Vanquish
b) Aston Martin DB9
c) Aston Martin Vantage N24

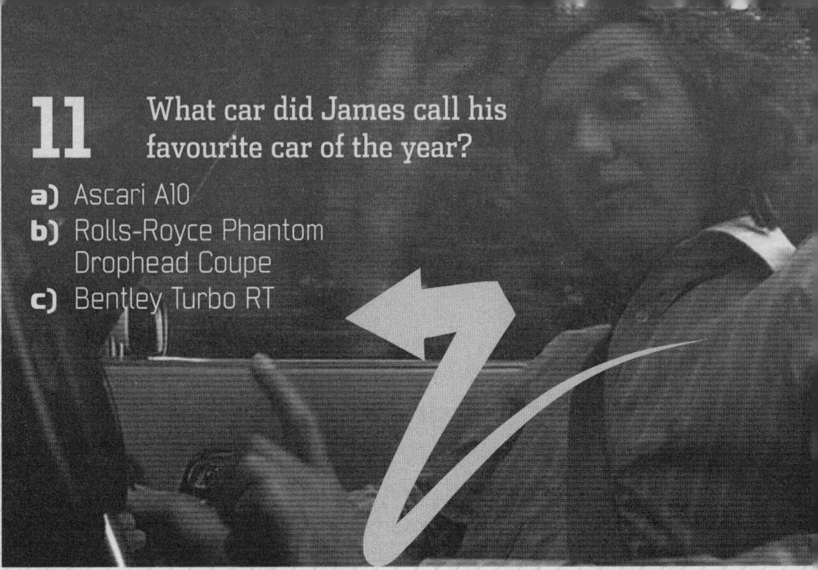

11 What car did James call his favourite car of the year?

a) Ascari A10
b) Rolls-Royce Phantom Drophead Coupe
c) Bentley Turbo RT

12 Who did James declare the winner of the African Challenge?

a) Richard's car 'Oliver'
b) His own car
c) Volkswagen Beetle

13 Which two words wasn't James allowed to use when reviewing the Alfa Romeo 159?

a) 'Power and soul' **b)** 'Passion and fun' **c)** 'Soul and passion'

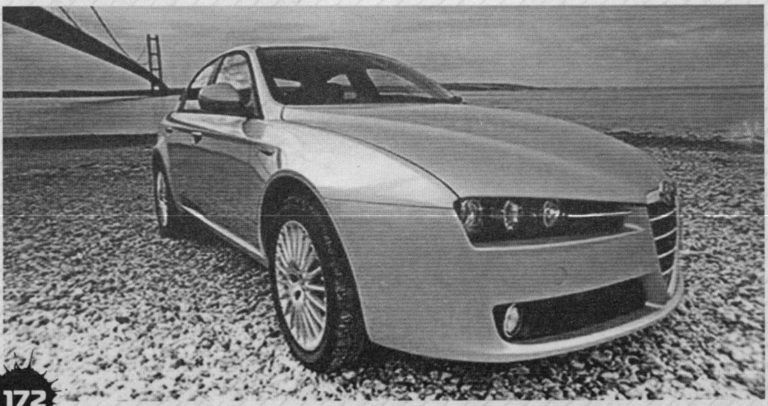

14 Who did James race against crossing the Humber river?

a) A man on rollerskates
b) A man who walked across the river
c) A man who rowed across the river

15 What happened in James' lap of the 24 Hour Endurance race?

a) He accelerated to over 50mph
b) He got lost
c) The turbo and clutch broke down

Answers

01 a) *The paint gun system didn't work that well.*
02 a) *He still couldn't move it after an hour.*
03 b) *He really, really doesn't.*
04 a) *James owns a Porsche Boxster.*
05 b) *Captain Slow was ecstatic to drive that fast.*
06 b) *Pagani Zonda F Roadster. And he liked it.*
07 c) *James really let out a Jeremy style yell.*
08 c) *Finland. It was very cold but they do good driving lessons.*
09 a), b) & c) *James' Triumph Herald was a disaster.*
10 c) *Possibly one of the most uncomfortable rides he's ever had.*
11 b) *The Rolls-Royce had style and grace.*
12 c) *The Beetle made it across Botswana with no problems at all.*
13 c) *James had a swear box if he used those words.*
14 b) *The man who walked across won the race.*
15 c) *The biofuel they used had eaten away the seals.*

Scores

11-15: *Just like James you were thorough and knowledgeable. Well done.*
6-10: *You might've taken a wrong turn at some point, just like Captain Slow does occasionally.*
0-5: *You flew through the questions too fast. Slow down and do it properly, like James.*

Who Said That?

Was it Jeremy, Richard or James?

Part 4

01

When someone says the name 'Ferrari Daytona', even if you haven't **seen** one you know with a name like that, it's **not** going to be a minger.

02

Let's get into the car's computer and make sure we've got the right settings. There's **sport**, dynamic, or **James May**.

03

I've **got** to beat Jeremy. I **cannot** be beaten by Jeremy.

04

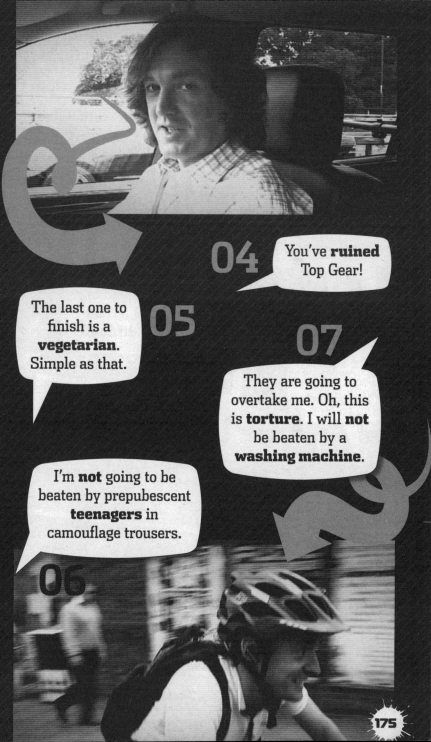

You've **ruined** Top Gear!

05

The last one to finish is a **vegetarian**. Simple as that.

07

They are going to overtake me. Oh, this is **torture**. I will **not** be beaten by a **washing machine**.

06

I'm **not** going to be beaten by prepubescent **teenagers** in camouflage trousers.

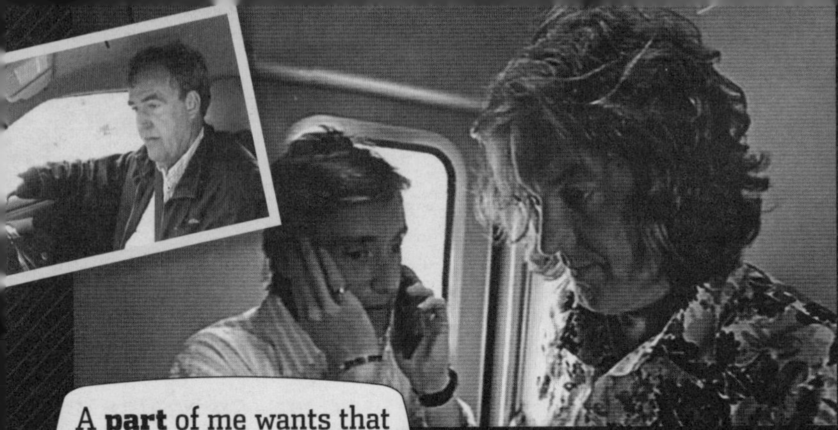

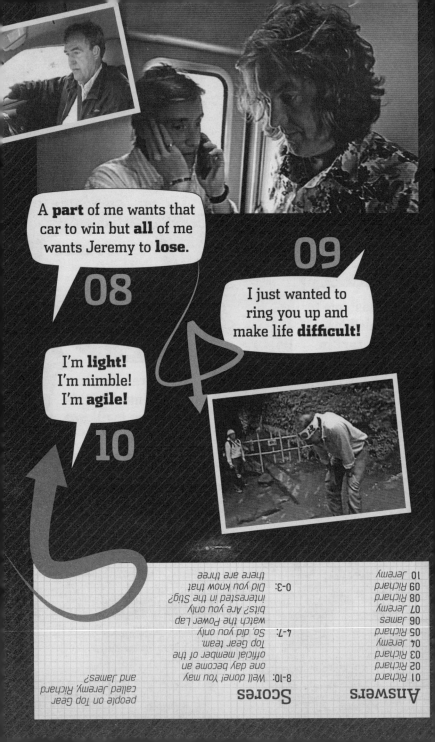

A **part** of me wants that car to win but **all** of me wants Jeremy to **lose.**

08

09

I just wanted to ring you up and make life **difficult!**

I'm **light!** I'm nimble! I'm **agile!**

10

Answers

01 Richard
02 Richard
03 Richard
04 Jeremy
05 Richard
06 James
07 Jeremy
08 Richard
09 Richard
10 Jeremy

Scores

8-10: *Well done! You may one day become an official member of the Top Gear team.*

4-7: *So, did you only watch the Power Lap bits? Are you only interested in the Stig?*

0-3: *Did you know that there are three people on Top Gear called Jeremy, Richard and James?*

THE RACES

One of our favourite things to do on *Top Gear* is to have an unusual race where the car has only a chance of winning. Do you remember who won when James drove a Peugeot 207 against parkour experts? And what about the race across Japan with Jeremy driving a Nissan GT-R and James and Richard in a Japanese bullet train?

01 Powerboat vs Ferrari

In Portofino, Italy, James jumped into a high-tech powerboat and raced Richard in a classic Ferrari to see who could reach their destination, Saint-Tropez, first, and be the winner.

TRUE/FALSE

02 Powerboat vs Ferrari

When James was flying along in the powerboat, the water became so rough and the boat bounced so violently up and down on the waves that the camera broke... and James nearly did, too.

TRUE/FALSE

03 Nissan GT-R vs Bullet Train

James and Richard climbed aboard a few bullet trains while Jeremy powered across Japan in a Nissan GT-R in a race to Nokogiri Yama where there is a Buddha shrine to road safety. **TRUE / FALSE**

04 Nissan GT-R vs Bullet Train

When James and Richard were on a bullet train, they managed to get separated because Richard went to find a drink and the trains split in half.

TRUE / FALSE

05 Audi RS6 vs French skiers

The Audi RS6 Richard drove in the race against the French skiers had more bhp than a Ferrari F430. **TRUE / FALSE**

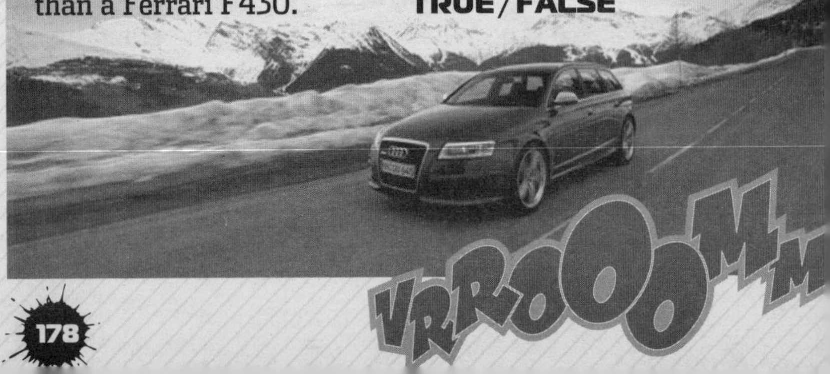

06 Audi RS5 vs French skiers

The huge power of the Audi RS6 enabled Richard to beat the French downhill skiers to the finish line by more than ten seconds. **TRUE / FALSE**

07 Fiat 500 vs BMX

James raced two BMX riders through the streets of Prague to see if a little Fiat on four wheels could beat two boys on two wheels. **TRUE / FALSE**

08 Fiat 500 vs BMX

The BMX riders managed to lose to James in his Fiat 500 because one of the riders crashed and fell off. **TRUE / FALSE**

09 Mercedes GL 500 vs bicycle vs racing boat vs public transport

The Stig didn't really seem to get the idea of public transport – not only did he not pay, he tried to drive the bus as well.

TRUE / FALSE

10 Mercedes GL 500 vs bicycle vs racing boat vs public transport

It was a very close race through London's rush hour. The very essence of *Top Gear* was ruined when Richard won on a bike and James came last in a car.

TRUE / FALSE

This is the **best** race in history!

11 Bugatti Veyron vs Eurofighter Typhoon

When Richard went up against a Eurofighter Typhoon, he was feeling a little bit nervous because he wasn't sure if the Bugatti Veyron would win. **TRUE/FALSE**

12 Bugatti Veyron vs Eurofighter Typhoon

The race between the Veyron and the fighter jet was a four mile race. The jet would fly vertically up into the air two miles and then back to the finish line and the Veyron would drive two miles then turn around back to the finish line. **TRUE/FALSE**

13 Peugeot 207 vs parkour experts

In the race across Liverpool, Captain Slow managed to not get lost and was rather pleased with himself. **TRUE / FALSE**

14 Peugeot 207 vs parkour experts

The parkour chaps jumped, ran and rolled to victory. They made it to the top of the Liver Building before James arrived at the bottom – in the Peugeot he wasn't happy with. **TRUE / FALSE**

15 Porsche Cayenne Turbo S vs parachutist

Richard was beaten in a race in Cyprus against a man who was wearing a suit that was modelled on a flying squirrel. **TRUE / FALSE**

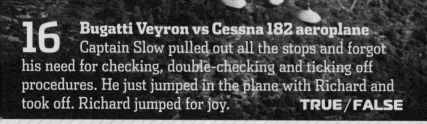

16 Bugatti Veyron vs Cessna 182 aeroplane

Captain Slow pulled out all the stops and forgot his need for checking, double-checking and ticking off procedures. He just jumped in the plane with Richard and took off. Richard jumped for joy. **TRUE / FALSE**

17 Audi RS4 vs speed climbers

Jeremy was certain he wasn't going to be beaten by a man with a hairband. But he was wrong. The climber made it to the top of the cliff with minutes to spare. **TRUE / FALSE**

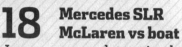

18 Mercedes SLR McLaren vs boat

Jeremy was so determined to win the race against James and Richard that he drove over 1,000 miles from London to Oslo without stopping. **TRUE / FALSE**

19 Ferrari 612 Scaglietti vs jet plane

Even though Richard and James were travelling at 500mph on a plane, Jeremy still managed to beat them to Verbier in his Ferrari, which had a top speed of 195mph.

TRUE / FALSE

20 Aston Martin DB9 vs train

In the race to Monte Carlo, Jeremy was pulled over by the French police for not driving fast enough!

TRUE / FALSE

Answers

01 **False.** *Richard drove a 40-year old Ferrari Daytona.*
02 **True.** *James was indeed broken by being bounced around.*
03 **True.** *Much to the disappointment of Richard and James, Jeremy won.*
04 **True.** *Richard was very, very worried.*
05 **True.** *The Audi RS6 has 572bhp.*
06 **False.** *The skiers beat Richard to the finish line.*
07 **False.** *The race was in Budapest.*
08 **False.** *The BMXers won the race against James.*
09 **False.** *The Stig was very well behaved on all the public transport. Good Stig.*
10 **True.** *Richard cycled like a maniac but he did win.*
11 **True.** *Richard was the only Top Gear presenter to not have driven the Bugatti and he wanted to do a good job.*
12 **False.** *The race was 2 miles long.*
13 **False.** *Surprisingly, James managed to get lost.*
14 **True.** *James did lose this race and in a car he didn't like. Poor James.*
15 **True.** *The flying squirrel won the race.*
16 **False.** *James was, and always will be, Captain Slow.*
17 **True.** *Jeremy was beaten twice when the climber parachuted back down the mountain.*
18 **False.** *Jeremy had to sleep for a few hours to recharge.*
19 **True.** *Jeremy was very, very smug about winning this race.*
20 **True.** *Jeremy had to put his foot down and go faster.*

Scores

16-20: *You're a bit competitive, aren't you? You love nothing more than a good race, right?*
8-15: *Maybe you're quick off the starting line but go too hard, too soon?*
0-7: *When someone says, 'ready, set, go', that means it's a race, okay?*

VIETNAM

SPECIAL PART 2

So, we're halfway through the journey from South to North Vietnam. There's been lots of rain, lots of breakdowns and more than a few cross words from Jeremy. Do you remember what else happened?

01 One of the most surprising things on the journey was finding one of the most perfect coast roads in the world. **TRUE / FALSE**

02 When Jeremy's bike broke down again, it was time for James and Richard to present him with their present – a large hand-painted portrait of Jeremy himself. **TRUE / FALSE**

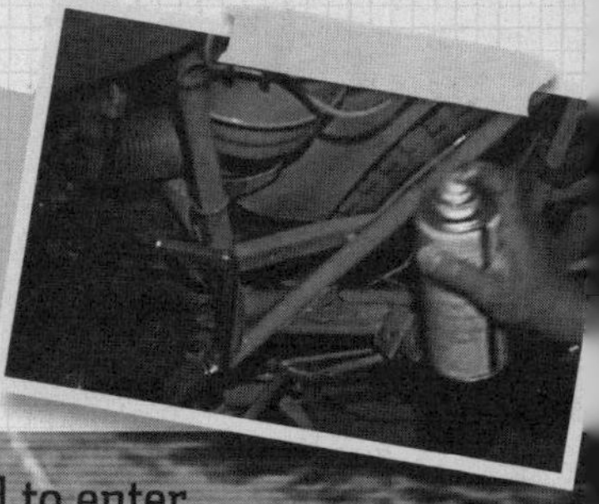

03 It was time to play another practical joke on Richard so James and Jeremy spray painted Richard's bike, with the help of some of the locals. **TRUE/FALSE**

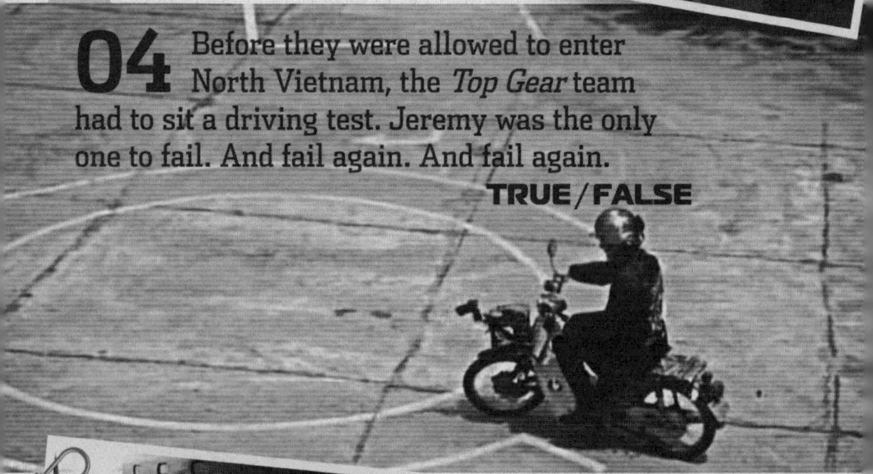

04 Before they were allowed to enter North Vietnam, the *Top Gear* team had to sit a driving test. Jeremy was the only one to fail. And fail again. And fail again. **TRUE/FALSE**

05 Jeremy realised that the only way to reach their destination in time was to cheat. Richard and James agreed so they chartered a bus with a trailer and jumped on. **TRUE/FALSE**

06 Their plan for cheating backfired when they ended up in the completely wrong city. After a thirteen-hour overnight journey, Jeremy and Richard tried hard not to get cross at James. **TRUE/FALSE**

07 Richard's favourite part of the journey was eating all the local delicacies. He especially enjoyed the snake and the sparrow. **TRUE/FALSE**

08 Jeremy really embraced the whole motorcycle idea and felt very happy. Then he fell off. **TRUE/FALSE**

09 When they arrived at the final destination of Ha Long, there was just one more challenge. Their bikes now had to be turned into water-ready jet skis, ready to sail on the bay. **TRUE/FALSE**

10 The winner of the challenge was surprisingly James. Jeremy sank and Richard's jet ski fell apart. James was very happy and sat gloating watching the sunset. **TRUE/FALSE**

Answers

01 **True.** *They all sat and admired the coastline and Jeremy felt the hairs stand up on the back of his neck.*
02 **False.** *The painting was of a Vietnamese boat scene.*
03 **True.** *Richard was very cranky that his beloved bike had been painted pink.*
04 **True.** *Jeremy was just not very good at steering a motorcycle.*
05 **False.** *They decided to catch a train.*
06 **False.** *Richard and James were cross with Jeremy as it was his fault they ended up in the wrong city.*
07 **False.** *Richard couldn't face any of the interesting food offerings and stuck to rice.*
08 **True.** *Poor Jeremy had a few scratches and bruises but he just got back on the bike and kept going.*
09 **True.** *They worked all night and were ready to go the next morning.*
10 **False.** *James' sank, Richard's lost steering and Jeremy's made it to the finishing line first.*

Scores

8-10: *A stellar effort. Congratulations! You did as well as the people who painted Richard's bike.*
4-7: *A good effort. You tried hard – about as hard as Jeremy tried to get them all on the right train.*
0-3: *As poor an effort as Jeremy mending James' stone statue with sticky tape.*

Top Gear Test Track

The *Top Gear* test track has seen its fair share of thrills, spills and appalling driving skills. And of course some of the best driving, when The Stig is in charge. What do you know?

01 Approximately how long is the *Top Gear* test track?

a) 2 miles
b) 2.5 miles
c) 3 miles

02 Who helped the *Top Gear* team design the *Top Gear* test track?

a) The Stig **b)** Lotus **c)** BMW

03 Who is the fastest female Star in a Reasonably-Priced Lacetti?

a) Jennifer Saunders
b) Keira Knightley
c) Dame Ellen MacArthur

04 Who is the fastest male Star in a Reasonably-Priced Lacetti?

a) Jay Kay
b) Jimmy Carr
c) Simon Cowell

05 Why is it called Gambon Corner?

a) Sir Michael Gambon didn't even make it round the corner
b) Sir Michael Gambon did it on 2 wheels
c) Sir Michael Gambon rolled his car

06 What is the fastest non-qualifying vehicle on the lap board?

a) Aston Martin DBRS
b) Caparo T1
c) BAE Sea Harrier

07 Who is at the top of the F1 leader board?

a) Sebastian Vettel
b) Lewis Hamilton
c) Nigel Mansell

08 What does MM mean when it's written beside a lap time?

a) Mildly moronic
b) Mildly moist
c) Mostly moist

09 How much time is assumed to be lost if the track is wet for a lap time?

a) 2.5 seconds **b)** 3 seconds **c)** 4 seconds

10 How much time is lost if the track is hot for a lap time?

a) 1 second **b)** No time at all **c)** 2 seconds

Answers

01 a) It's 1.75 miles long to be exact
02 b) Lotus designed the test track as a test of all the aspects of a car and driver.
03 a) Jennifer Saunders did it in 1 minute 46.1 seconds.
04 a) Jay Kay did it in 1 minute 45.88 seconds.
05 b) Sir Michael Gambon was lucky he didn't roll.
06 c) The BAE Sea Harrier made in 0.31.2 seconds.
07 a) Sebastian Vettel.
08 b) The track is a little wet.
09 c) A wet track is 4 seconds slower than a dry one.
10 c) Hot or humid conditions cost a driver 2 seconds.

Scores

8-10: You know the track so well you could draw it with your eyes shut.
4-7: Where do you think you'd go on the Star in a Reasonably Priced Car board? I'd say somewhere near Jimmy Carr – he spun off the track.
0-3: There's a track on a show called Top Gear. And many people do laps around it. In cars.

THE CHALLENGES

Top Gear love a challenge. Especially when it involves competing against each other whilst driving ridiculous cars, boats and motorhomes in extreme weather conditions. Do you remember who won, who lost and who got lost in these challenges?

01 What was the first challenge the *Top Gear* team had to do when they bought a lorry each?

a) Complete a lorry driving test
b) Decorate their lorries
c) Change the tyres

02 A challenge for the lorry drivers was to do power slides. What happened to Jeremy when he tried to complete the challenge?

a) He sneakily got The Stig's lorry driving cousin to do it for him
b) He fell off his seat and injured himself
c) He shredded the tyres in a cloud of smoke

03 At the start of the race from Basel to Blackpool, Jeremy could see a big problem. What was it?

a) They weren't allowed to modify their cars
b) They had to travel in the same car
c) Their fuel tanks weren't big enough

04 What car did James choose to drive in the Basel to Blackpool race?

a) His beloved Fiat Panda
b) VW Golf GTi
c) Subaru Legacy Diesel

05 When James and Jeremy drove a modified Toyota Hilux to the North Pole, what practical joke did Jeremy like to play?

a) Shout at James that there was a polar bear behind him
b) Drive off when James was sitting on 'the throne' attached to the tow bar
c) Drive off and leave James standing in the snow

06 What extra bit of kit did Richard's dog sled team use to travel a little bit faster?

a) A snowmobile for Richard to drive when the dogs were tired
b) An extra few huskies that replaced tired dogs
c) A kite that towed Mattie

07 In the Miami to New Orleans $1,000 car challenge, the Top Gear team had to brake as hard as they could before they hit... what?

a) A creek full of alligators
b) A creek full of piranhas
c) A big tree

08 Another challenge on the Miami to New Orleans road trip was to only be able to eat what they found on the side of the road. What did they find?

a) A squirrel **b)** A tortoise **c)** An alligator

09 When the *Top Gear* team were qualifying for the 24 Hour race, what happened?

a) Jeremy shouted himself hoarse screaming at the other drivers
b) Richard was too short and couldn't see out the windscreen
c) James couldn't count and only did 2 of his 3 laps

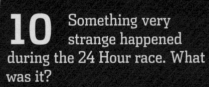

10 Something very strange happened during the 24 Hour race. What was it?

a) The Stig looked for a moment like he might speak
b) James overtook someone
c) Jeremy was nice to someone

11 What present did James buy for himself when he was driving his 'gentleman's racer' on the *Top Gear* quest to find the perfect road?

a) A fan **b)** A pillow **c)** Some fluffy dice

12 Richard picked where he thought the best driving road in the world would be... but there was one little problem. What was it?

a) There was a bicycle race blocking the road
b) There was a herd of cows blocking the road
c) There was a rally car race so the road was closed

13 On the way to take their amphibious vehicles across the English Channel, disaster struck. What happened?

a) James' Herald mast got caught going under a bridge
b) Jeremy's Nissank caught on fire
c) Richard's Damper Van blew up

14 How many times did James end up in the water in his attempt to leave Dover?

a) Twice
b) Three times
c) Four times

15

One of the challenges in Africa was to drive through a wildlife park full of lions, tigers, hippos and crocodiles. What protection did Jeremy have on his car?

a) Chicken wire **b)** Drink cans **c)** Tarpaulin

16

What practical joke did Jeremy and Richard play on James during the Africa challenge?

a) Put a cow's head in James' tent
b) Hid a fish under his driving seat
c) Put a piece of steak on top of his engine

17

Before the motorhome motor sport racing event, what did James do?

a) Lighten his motorhome by stripping it of its interior
b) Paint his motorhome with racing stripes
c) Cook a pie with gravy and vegetables

18

Motorhome racing was one of Richard's inventions. What place did he come in the first – and perhaps only – race?

a) First **b)** Third **c)** Last

19 What did James do when he was doing a lap during the Leyland £1,200 Challenge?

a) Took a wrong turning
b) Got lost on the track
c) Failed to reach 60mph

20 A near miracle happened during the water test for the Leyland £1,200 Challenge. What was it?

a) Jeremy came to the rescue when Richard's car overheated
b) Jeremy won the challenge and wasn't smug
c) James lapped Richard

Answers

01 b) *They all went for very different decorating themes.*
02 b) *Poor Jeremy cut himself and had an incident with the gear lever.*
03 c) *Theoretically, none of them would travel 750 miles on a single tank.*
04 c) *James was very sensible and chose a diesel.*
05 b) *James did not enjoy being disturbed when he was on the throne.*
06 c) *Mattie skied with the kite ahead and this encouraged the dogs.*
07 a) *Richard just managed to not end up being eaten by an alligator.*
08 a) *Richard refused to skin the squirrel. Don't blame him, really.*
09 c) *James had to jump back in and do another lap.*
10 b) *James was overjoyed when he overtook someone.*
11 b) *A pillow for his sore bottom. The suspension was brutal.*
12 a) *The bicycle race really slowed the team down.*
13 b) *Jeremy had filled his engine with foam – which caught fire.*
14 b) *The last time he even had a cup of tea while floating in his life jacket.*
15 b) *A wall of drink cans was made to block up the big gap the missing door left.*
16 a) *The cow's head was mistakenly put in Richard's own tent. Whoops.*
17 c) *James made himself a hearty meal.*
18 b) *Richard came a decent placed third.*
19 b) *James had to turn around and take the correct corner.*
20 c) *James did indeed lap Richard because his Leyland retained water the longest.*

Scores

16-20: *If there ever is a challenge announced, you'll be first in line to try something stupid.*
8-15: *Did you go into a daydream, thinking up your own challenges when the Top Gear ones were on?*
0-7: *Is it because you think the challenges are stupid or is it because you are... stupid?*

HOW HARD CAN IT BE?

***T**op Gear* are always confident about how easy everything looks... until they try it, and it usually ends in disaster. So let's see if you can get all these questions right. How hard can it be?

01 The *Top Gear* team decided to make their own stretch limos. And Richard also tried to create the world's first roadster limousine. **TRUE / FALSE**

02 James decided to show what a true genius he was and used two cars to create his limousine. **TRUE / FALSE**

03 Jeremy and James both set fire to their stretch limousines when they were building them. **TRUE / FALSE**

04 Jeremy really messed up assembling the Caterham. He put one seat in backwards. **TRUE / FALSE**

05 When the chaps tried to put the engine into their Caterham, it went in perfectly.

TRUE/FALSE

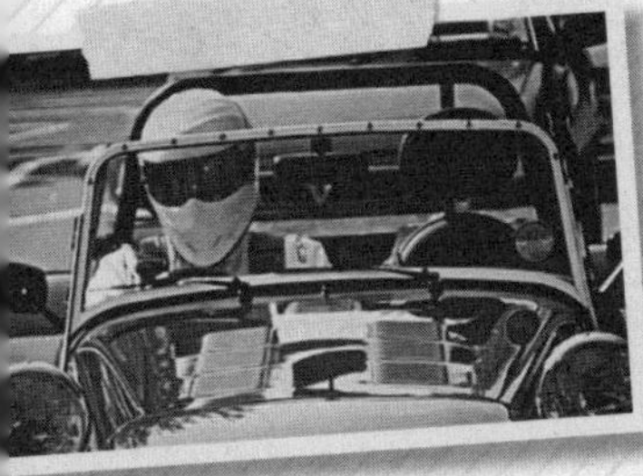

06 Jeremy, James and Richard lost to The Stig in the Caterham challenge.

TRUE/FALSE

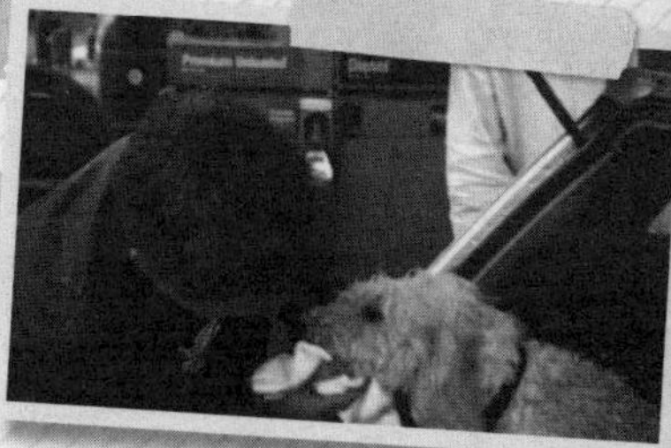

07 During the drive on the caravanning holiday, Richard got car sick and threw up. **TRUE/FALSE**

08 James crashed the caravan into a pole when leaving the petrol station. **TRUE/FALSE**

09 When they went to launch the Reliant Robin space shuttle, it was the largest rocket to be launched in Britain. **TRUE / FALSE**

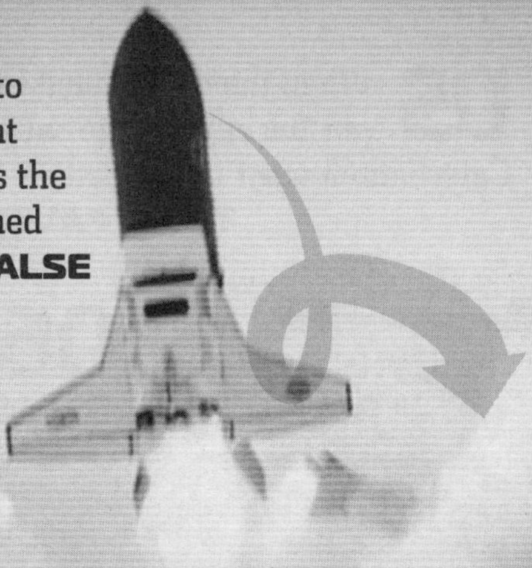

10 When Richard was doing research for the Reliant Robin he crashed a model aeroplane. **TRUE / FALSE**

11 The first challenge in growing their own petrol was to park their tractors in the *Top Gear* car park. **TRUE / FALSE**

12 In the Grow Your Own Petrol challenge, Richard's tractor was the slowest around the *Top Gear* test track, and so won the challenge. **TRUE / FALSE**

13 Jeremy towed a massive aeroplane with his tractor in the drag race for the Grow Your Own Petrol challenge. **TRUE/FALSE**

14 When the *Top Gear* team decided to race to the North Pole, they were the first to attempt it in a car. **TRUE/FALSE**

15 The tyres used on the Toyota Hilux to drive to the North Pole were handmade. **TRUE/FALSE**

Answers

01 True. *And it wasn't weather proof.*
02 True. *And it was spectacular. Sort of.*
03 False. *Jeremy and Richard set fire to their stretch limos.*
04 True. *Jeremy had to take the seat out and start again.*
05 False. *They knocked the car body off its support.*
06 False. *They only beat The Stig because he was stopped by the police.*
07 False. *Top Gear Dog got car sick and threw up.*
08 True. *James got irritable when Jeremy and Richard teased him.*
09 True. *It crashed spectacularly well too.*
10 True. *Richard crashed it into a shed.*
11 False. *They had to reverse their tractors out of the carpark.*
12 True. *The slowest tractor won.*
13 True. *James won the challenge.*
14 True. *And we know why it wasn't that much fun.*
15 True. *Handmade, and massive.*

Scores

11-15: *You know that just like the Top Gear team thinks, anything is possible!*
6-10: *Just like the Top Gear team, you give everything a go, but don't always get it right.*
0-5: *You would prefer a nice cup of tea and a lie down rather than trying out strange experiments.*

Ridiculously Hard ?s

01 What is the name of the first corner of the *Top Gear* test track?

a) Crooner Curve **b)** Chicago Corner **c)** Bentley Bend

02 What is the name of the last corner of the *Top Gear* test track?

a) Wilson Bend **b)** Bacharach Bend **c)** Gambon Corner

03 What was the type of motorcycle Richard bought in Vietnam?

a) Mumpt **b)** Minsk **c)** Minschke

04 What was the colour of the motorcycle James bought in Vietnam?

a) Green **b)** Blue **c)** Red

05 What did James use to saw his car in half to make a stretch limousine?

a) Chainsaw
b) Plasma cutter
c) Laser cutter

06 What had to happen next after the Caterham engine had been dropped into the car?

a) The brakes had to be connected
b) The starter motor had to be fixed
c) Petrol had to be added into the fuel tank

07 What was the top speed the Kia could reach towing the caravan the *Top Gear* team took on holiday?

a) 60mph **b)** 30mph **c)** 50mph

08 What else happened on the caravanning holiday that delayed their arrival at the campsite?

a) They got lost because James was navigating
b) The car got a flat tyre
c) They argued over who should be driving

09 How many tonnes of thrust were needed to launch the Reliant Robin into space?

a) Four
b) Five
c) Eight

10 What car did Richard reverse into in his tractor in the Grow Your Own Petrol challenge?

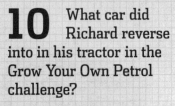

a) Koeniggsegg CCX
b) Vauxhall Astra Diesel
c) Porsche 911

11 What was the slowest lap time around the *Top Gear* test track by a tractor?

a) 4 minutes 35 seconds
b) 4 minutes 49 seconds
c) 5 minutes 2 seconds

12 How many cars did James tow in the Grow Your Own Petrol challenge tractor drag race?

a) Seven **b)** Nine **c)** Five

13 Which supercar won the fuel economy challenge?

a) Audi R8
b) Aston Martin DBS
c) Ferrari 599

14 What is the slowest Power Lap time around the *Top Gear* track?

a) 1 minute 42 seconds
b) 1 minute 46 seconds
c) 1 minute 52 seconds

15 How fast did the Koenigsegg CCX (with *Top Gear* spoiler) go in a Power Lap?

a) 1 minute 17.4 seconds
b) 1 minute 17.6 seconds
c) 1 minute 16.5 seconds

Answers

01 a) *Crooner Corner.*
02 c) *Gambon Corner.*
03 b) *Richard bought a Russian-built Minsk.*
04 a) *Green.*
05 b) *Plasma cutter – to make precision cuts.*
06 a) *Many things had to happen but the brakes were first.*
07 b) *The poor Kia didn't have enough power for the caravan.*
08 b) *It took twenty minutes to change the tyre.*
09 c) *A whopping eight tonnes of thrust.*
10 b) *The Astra was a prototype.*
11 b) *Richard's was so slow they even had a cup of tea.*
12 a) *James dragged the amphibious cars and a few others he found lying around.*
13 a) *The Audi managed five miles at top speed on one gallon of petrol.*
14 b) *The Aston DB5 is much slower than you'd think.*
15 b) *1 minute 17.6 seconds.*

Scores

11-15: *That's it. You've made it. You're now an honorary member of the Top Gear team.*
6-10: *Fantastic effort. Maybe you should try for a presenter's job next time there's an audition.*
0-5: *Oh dear. Do you just like looking at the pretty cars with the volume down?*

TopGear
PRODUCTION OFFICE

BUGATTI

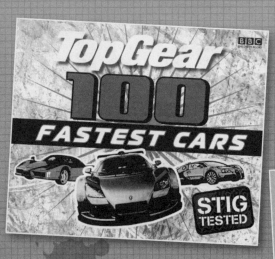

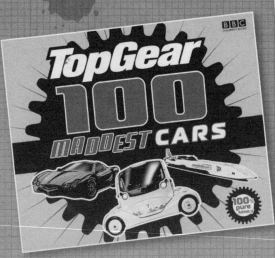